English

YEAR 4

Victoria Burrill

GALORE PARK

AN HACHETTE UK COMPANY

The Publishers would like to thank the following for permission to reproduce copyright material.

Photo credits p3 © CCI/REX/Shutterstock **p10** © Alexey Kljatov/Shutterstock.com **p18** © Rawpixel.com/Shutterstock.com **p22** © Ivan abornev/Shutterstock.com **p28** © UPP/TopFoto **p33** © Iconics/a.collectionRF/Getty Images **p42** © Herschel Hoffmeyer/Shutterstock.com **p48** © Herschel Hoffmeyer/Shutterstock.com **p53** © Pictorial Press Ltd/Alamy Stock Photo **p57** © Erica Finstad and Atikinka/Shutterstock.com **p59** © Atikinka/Shutterstock.com **p64** © Leonid Andronov/iStock/Thinkstock/Getty Images **p69** © Dieter Spears/istockphoto **p75** © Rowlandson/Shutterstock **p83** © Imagestate Media (John Foxx)/Vol 12 Nature & Animals 2 **p90** © Take Photo/Shutterstock.com **p94** © Samuel Cohen/Shutterstock.com **p100** © Earl Robbins/Fotolia **p106** © Sean Gladwell/Fotolia **p113** © JENS WOLF/dpa picture alliance archive/Alamy Stock Photo **p118** © Milkovasa/Shutterstock.com

Acknowledgements p3 *NONE, STORYBKS-TALES BROTHRS GRIMM HCR 86, 1st* Ed., ©1992. Reprinted by permission of Pearson Education, Inc., New York, New York. **p5** 'Snow facts' adapted from www.metoffice.gov.uk (public domain) **p15** Morpurgo, M. (2012). Kensuke's Kingdom. Used by permission from David Higham Associates. **p17** Taylor, T. (2014). The Cay. London: Penguin **p27** 'Roald Dahl's days' from www.roalddahl.com (used with permission) **p30** Dahl, R. (2016). James and the Giant Peach. Penguin **p40** Stilgoe, Richard. Brilliant The Dinosaur (1995). Reproduced with kind permission of Pavilion Books Company Limited. **p41** 'Eyewitness Guides: Dinosaur' by David Norman and Angela Milner (2003), pages 20–21. Reproduced by permission of Penguin Books Ltd. **p50** From *The Silver Sword* by Ian Serraillier. Published by *Jonathan Cape*. Reprinted by permission of The Random House Group Limited. **p53** Excerpt(s) from THE DIARY OF A YOUNG GIRL: THE DEFINITIVE EDITION by Anne Frank, edited by Otto H. Frank and Mirjam Pressler, translated by Susan Massotty, translation copyright © 1995 by Doubleday, a division of Random House LLC. Used by permission of Doubleday, an imprint of the Knopf Doubleday Publishing Group, a division of Penguin Random House LLC. All rights reserved. Any third party use of this material, outside of this publication, is prohibited. Interested parties must apply directly to Penguin Random House LLC for permission. (permission sought for UK and Commonwealth) **p61** *The Railway Children* by E. Nesbit (public domain) **p63** 'All About Trains' by Michael Harris published by Anness Publishing Ltd. (used with permission) **p75** 'Snail' from *The Iron Wolf* by Ted Hughes, published by Faber & Faber Ltd (permission sought) **p75** © Judith Nicholls 1987, from MIDNIGHT FOREST by Judith Nicholls, pub. Faber & Faber, reprinted by permission of the author. **p76** 'Lobster' from The Iron Wolf by Ted Hughes, published by Faber & Faber Ltd (permission obtained for World excluding US. Permission sought for US) **p76** 'Birds' by Irene Rawnsley (permission sought) **p87** King, C. (2010). Stig of the Dump. Penguin UK. Used by permission of David Higham Associates. **p100** *The Water Babies* by Charles Kingsley (public domain) **p101** 'They Call to One Another' by George Barker. Used with permission from Elspeth Barker. **p111** *The Iron Man* by Ted Hughes, published by Faber & Faber Ltd (permission obtained for World excluding US. Permission sought for US)

Every effort has been made to trace all copyright holders, but if any have been inadvertently overlooked, the Publishers will be pleased to make the necessary arrangements at the first opportunity.

Although every effort has been made to ensure that website addresses are correct at time of going to press, Galore Park cannot be held responsible for the content of any website mentioned in this book. It is sometimes possible to find a relocated web page by typing in the address of the home page for a website in the URL window of your browser.

Hachette UK's policy is to use papers that are natural, renewable and recyclable products and made from wood grown in sustainable forests. The logging and manufacturing processes are expected to conform to the environmental regulations of the country of origin.

Orders: **Teachers** please contact Bookpoint Ltd, 130 Park Drive, Milton Park, Abingdon, Oxon OX14 4SE. Telephone: (44) 01235 400555. Email: primary@bookpoint.co.uk Lines are open from 9 a.m. to 5 p.m., Monday to Saturday, with a 24-hour message answering service.

Parents, Tutors please call: 020 3122 6405 (Monday to Friday, 9:30am – 4.30pm). Email: parentenquiries@galorepark.co.uk

Visit our website at www.galorepark.co.uk for details of other revision guides for Common Entrance, examination papers and Galore Park publications.

ISBN: 9781471882128

© Victoria Burrill 2017
First published in 2017 by
Galore Park Publishing Ltd,
An Hachette UK Company
Carmelite House
50 Victoria Embankment
London EC4Y 0DZ
www.galorepark.co.uk

Impression number   10 9 8 7 6 5 4 3 2 1
Year   2021 2020 2019 2018 2017

Cover photo © Tatiana Kalashnikova /123RF.com

Typeset in India
Printed in Italy

A catalogue record for this title is available from the British Library.

Contents

Introduction

Reading unlocks the world. Reading newspaper and magazine articles provides you with valuable information about what is going on around you, reading letters and diary extracts allows you to share the thoughts and experiences of other people, and reading stories and poems unlocks your imagination and lets you fly freely to places, spaces and times you may never be able to visit in real life. And being able to retrieve and summarise what you have read, to understand the structure and purpose of a text and why an author has used the language they have used, and to infer meaning and make deductions from what you have read are the keys to reading. In turn, reading helps you learn how to speak, how to listen and how to write; how to communicate your own thoughts, feelings and ideas with those around you.

This series adopts a skills-based approach to teaching English. This means that you will be introduced to a skill, such as the comprehension skill of inference or how to write a descriptive passage, and you will return to it throughout Years 3 to 6, getting better and better at it over time.

⮕ Notes on features

Throughout this series you will come across the following features that are designed to help you:

Skill focus

This box will tell you which comprehension skill each chapter focuses on.

 This box points you to the reading list for each chapter. The reading lists can be found in *English Year 4 Answers* (available as a PDF download from the Galore Park website – ISBN 9781471896613).

In these boxes you will come across questions to help you:
- practise your comprehension skills
- practise using grammar correctly
- practise using punctuation correctly
- practise your spelling
- develop your vocabulary
- practise your creative writing skills.

Speaking and listening

These activities will help you develop your speaking and listening skills.

Snowy stories

There is something quite special about newly fallen snow. It is peaceful and beautiful, but it is also freezing cold, slippery and dangerous. For this reason, snowy settings make for super stories. Hopefully you will be inspired by these glittering winter wonderlands.

Skill focus: Retrieval

In this chapter you will learn how to read questions carefully to work out what you need to find in the text to answer them. It is really important to enjoy your reading and get involved in the stories, settings and characters that you come across. By learning to find your way around the text you will get even more enjoyment from the books you read.

A reading list of stories set in cold, snowy, wintery settings and non-fiction books about snow can be found in *English Year 4 Answers*.

Comprehension

When you are asked to find a piece of information in a text, you need to scan the passage to locate it. Scanning means reading something quickly, not reading every word. This is a particularly useful skill as the passages you read get longer because, after reading the passage, you may not be able to remember the answer and you will therefore have to find it. The first time you read the passage, you should read it in detail; you can scan the text more quickly when you are looking for the answers later on.

To find the answer to a question, you need to know what words or groups of words to look out for as you scan the text. The question should give you clues:

- Who ...? You are looking for a name, such as 'dog', 'grandmother' or 'Ranjit'.
- When ...? You are looking for a time, such as 'tomorrow' or 'two o'clock'.

- Where ...? You are looking for a place, such as 'my house' or 'Manchester'.
- What ...? You need to know the subject of the 'what'. Is it the weather, the time of year, an action, a feeling, etc.? This will determine what you scan for.

Take a look at this example:

> Yawning loudly, Oliver clumsily picked up his keys from the table. He fumbled in the cupboard for his football boots and finally left the house, just as the clock in the hallway was striking seven o'clock. He hated getting up so early, but for the big match he was prepared to do it!
>
> Outside, the grass was frosty and the cold bit at his skin as he walked briskly along the road. Christmas lights still twinkled outside many of the houses, giving off a colourful glow as he headed to the park. At the top of his street he spied Amal, his friend and the left winger for his team. He called out to him and they walked the rest of the way together, discussing tactics, the likelihood of winning and the way they would celebrate if they did actually win the cup.

1 When did Oliver leave the house? (1 mark)

The important word in the question is 'when'. It means you need to look for a time. Times usually have numbers in them or they are times of day (morning, lunchtime, etc.). You might also look for 'o'clock' or the words 'clock' or 'watch' if the character in the passage checks the time. The parts of the text highlighted in yellow will help you. Your answer might look like this:
Oliver left the house at 7 a.m. (1 mark)

2 At what time of the year does this passage take place? (1 mark)

Look for clues about the season or month. These might include information about the weather or seasonal events.

3 Who did Oliver meet on the way to the park? (2 marks)

Look for a name. For 2 marks you will need to name the person and explain their relationship to Oliver.

> Now try to answer questions 2 and 3 yourself.

Try the following comprehension exercise, using the guidance above to help you answer the questions. Questions that require you to scan the text and retrieve an answer are in bold.

Snow White

In this retelling of a well-known story, we learn how Snow White got her name.

It was the middle of winter and broad flakes of snow were tumbling and swirling around in the cold night air. Dark shadows crept into every nook and cranny and stood out sharply against
5   the pale silver glow reflected from the moonlit snowdrifts. The small creatures of the forest had taken refuge, huddling deep in their nests far below the frozen shroud that lay across the land.

High on a hill above the ice-latticed treetops
10   stood a castle. It rested like a great black rock amidst the gleaming whiteness that surrounded it. Its turrets and walls were dark and gloomy in the creaking chill, blind save for a solitary golden glow high up in one corner of its ebony
15   facade. The glow came from a tiny window and it flickered like a dying star as the snowflakes danced past it.

Close by the window sat a queen quietly sewing and looking out over the frosty scene. She had a
20   child within her whose birth was near, but despite the joy this brought her, there was a sadness in her heart. As she measured her stitches she prayed for strength, for the cold of the long winter had entered her bones and she felt frail and weak.

Suddenly, she started, as the sharp needle pierced her finger and three drops of blood
25   fell onto the snow-covered windowsill. She gazed thoughtfully at the crimson stains colouring the white snow and her sad eyes filled with tears.

'Would that my child be a daughter with skin as white as that snow, with cheeks as rosy red as blood and hair as ebony black as the window-frame.'

Outside the wind gusted wildly and the long night wore on.

30   The good queen died but her child was, indeed, a daughter. The queen had died that the child should live, but just before she closed her eyes for the last time she saw that her wish had come true – the child's skin was as fair as driven snow, her cheeks were rosy blood-red and her shining hair was as black as ebony. The queen's lips had trembled; 'I will call her Snow White,' she murmured.

From 'Snow White' in *Tales from the Brothers Grimm*, re-told by Robert Mathias

4 (a) What time of day is it at the beginning of the passage? (1 mark)

   (b) How do you know? (1 mark)

5 (a) What was the weather like at the start of the passage? (1 mark)

   (b) How do you know? (1 mark)

6 Where was the castle? (1 mark)

7 'it flickered like a dying star' (line 16). What does the word 'flickered' tell you about the light in the window? (1 mark)

8 (a) Where was the queen sitting? (1 mark)

   (b) What was the queen doing? (1 mark)

9 (a) What three things did the queen wish for her daughter? (3 marks)

   (b) Where did she get each idea from? (3 marks)

10 Do you think the story would make you feel differently if it were set in the summer? Explain your answer in a few sentences and refer to the text. (4 marks)

Speaking and listening

11 Sit in a circle as a class. Nominate someone to choose a topic and play the A to Z game. Topics could include: adjectives, alternative words for 'said', characters from books, authors. Go round the circle, taking it in turns to say a word that fits the topic. The first word must begin with 'a', the second with 'b' and so on.

Now try this comprehension exercise. It is based on a non-fiction passage, which you will need to scan to find information. Remember that you can use subheadings to help you find information too.

Snow facts

In this article, published by the Met Office, which monitors and measures the weather in the UK, you will learn some interesting facts about snow.

Snow is one of the most impressive displays of weather and it's also one of the most fascinating phenomena. In this article we walk you through facts you might not know about the white stuff, from the speed of snow to the chance of getting a white Christmas.

Deepest snow in the UK

5   The deepest snow ever recorded in an inhabited area of the UK was near Ruthin in North Wales during the severe winter of 1946–47. A series of cold spells brought large drifts of snow across the UK causing transport problems and fuel shortages. During March 1947 a snow depth of 1.65 metres was recorded.

It doesn't have to be freezing to snow

10   Generally, the air temperature does need to be at or below freezing for snow to fall. However, if rain falls continuously through air with a temperature as high as 6 °C, it may cause the air temperature to fall low enough for the rain to turn to snow. This is because rain that persists for some time will gradually cool the air that surrounds it.

The snowiest place in the UK

15   Scotland sees the most snow in the UK, with snow or sleet falling on 52 days on average. The weather station that recorded the most snowfall in the UK was the Cairngorm Chairlift with snow falling on 76 days throughout the year, making it the snowiest place in the UK.

Every snowflake is unique

20   Part of the enduring appeal of snowflakes is their intricate appearance, meaning that all snowflakes are unique. If you look closely at a snowflake you will see countless individual features, all of which formed ever so slightly differently owing to slight changes in the environment as it formed.

Snow isn't white

25   While snowflakes appear white as they fall through the sky or as they accumulate on the ground as snowfall, they are in fact totally clear.

The speed of snow

Most snow falls at a speed of between 1–4 mph dependent upon the individual snowflake's mass and surface area, as well as the environmental conditions
30   surrounding its descent.

Photographing snowflakes

The first person to capture a photograph of a snowflake was a farmer from the small town of Jericho in Vermont, USA. After years of experimenting with connecting microscopes to a camera, in 1885 Wilson Bentley succeeding in
35   capturing the first ever photograph of a snowflake. During his lifetime he photographed more than 5,000 snowflakes and even released a book packed with 2,400 images of snowflakes.

Chance of a white Christmas

Whilst the vision of a Christmas Day surrounded by snow fills Christmas cards,
40   movies and songs, snow is actually much more likely in January and February than in December. In the UK, snow or sleet falls on an average of 3.9 days in December, compared to 5.3 days in January, 5.6 days in February and 4.2 days in March. There has been a widespread covering of snow (over 40% of weather stations reporting snow) on Christmas Day only four times in the last 51 years.

Adapted from www.metoffice.gov.uk

---

12 (a) Where and when was the deepest snow ever recorded in the UK? (2 marks)

   (b) How deep was the snow? (1 mark)

13 What can cause snow, even when the air isn't at freezing point? (1 mark)

14 (a) Where exactly is the snowiest place in the UK? (1 mark)

   (b) For how many days did it snow there in one year? (1 mark)

15 What causes each snowflake to be unique? (1 mark)

16 (a) How did Wilson Bentley manage to photograph a snowflake for the first time? (2 marks)

   (b) Was this the only time he photographed a snowflake? How do you know? (2 marks)

17 Why is a white Christmas unlikely in the UK? Explain your answer fully. (2 marks)

Speaking and listening

18 Write a script for a short news report in which the announcer tells the audience that snowstorms have struck Britain, leaving motorists stranded and electricity cables broken. Present this news report to your class. Remember to read it like a newsreader. You could watch a news report or weather report on TV first so that you know how to speak and get ideas for what you might say.

→ Grammar

In this section you will learn to describe things using expanded noun phrases.

Expanded noun phrases

In order to make your writing more descriptive, you can use noun phrases. These are phrases in which a noun is joined by adjectives (describing words), prepositions (words showing direction or position) and other nouns. By using these in your writing, you help the reader to imagine more clearly the things that you are describing. You are painting a picture with your words. For example:

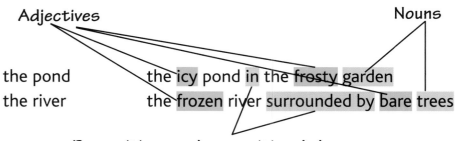

You can also make noun phrases with abstract nouns. Abstract nouns are nouns that you can't touch, hold or experience with your five senses. For example:

| peace | long-lasting, worldwide peace in every country |
| happiness | deep, true happiness from dawn until dusk |

19 Copy these extended noun phrases and then underline the prepositions and circle the adjectives.

(a) the whistling wind through the tall trees

(b) the woolly hat on the white snowman

(c) a jolly Santa with a bright red outfit

(d) colourful Christmas presents under the decorated tree

(e) the long, difficult walk over the steep, frosty mountain

20 Copy these nouns and add an appropriate adjective to each one.

(a) forest   (c) wind   (e) sky

(b) rain   (d) snow

21 Write an expanded noun phrase for each of these nouns. Add an adjective, a preposition and a further noun and adjective to them.

(a) ice   (c) lake   (e) scarf

(b) clouds   (d) children

Punctuation

In this section you will practise punctuating sentences with capital letters, full stops, exclamation marks and question marks.

Basic sentence punctuation

Here are some reminders to help you revise your basic sentence punctuation.

All sentences start with a capital letter. For example:

The snow fell gently from the sky.

Proper nouns (names of one-of-a-kind nouns) also need capital letters. For example:

My Uncle Bryan and Auntie Suzie spend Christmas Day on the beach in Australia.

All sentences end with a full stop, an exclamation mark or question mark. For example:

It snowed on my birthday.

Wow, snow!

Do you want to build a snowman?

---

22 Copy these sentences and add in the missing punctuation:

(a) will it snow on boxing day

(b) i put my hat and coat on because it was so cold

(c) it's freezing

(d) the trees are bare in winter

(e) playing in the snow is paul's favourite thing about january

23 Copy out this passage and add in all of the missing sentence punctuation:

when is your favourite time of year is it summer july and august are warm and you can play outdoors late into the evening while the sun shines is it autumn the leaves begin to fall and change into beautiful colours is it spring the flowers begin to bloom and the days start to get longer or is it winter everybody hopes for snow so that they can build snowmen and have snowball fights wow every season is so different

---

Spelling

In this section you will learn to spell words ending in the suffix -ation.

The suffix -ation is used to turn a verb into a noun. For example:

inform + ation → information

If the verb ends in a consonant, just add -ation. If the verb ends in an -e or a -y, remove the -e or the -y, then add -ation. For example:

occupy + ation → occupation

adore + ation → adoration

24 Add the suffix -ation to these verbs.

    (a) imagine   **(c)** explore   **(e)** confirm

    (b) consider   **(d)** combine

25 Add the suffix -ation to these verbs and use the new word in a sentence.

    (a) sense   **(c)** admire   **(e)** inspire

    (b) prepare   **(d)** starve

Vocabulary

When you write a story or a description, describing the weather is a good way to set the mood. If you describe it in detail it can help to build a picture of the setting in the reader's mind. Here are some different types of weather you might describe:

| sun | heat | wind | rain | thunder | lightning | hail | mist |
| fog | cloud | sleet | snow | storm | drizzle | gale | blizzard |

Think about the different moods they might create. A sunny day feels happier than a misty morning, which sounds more mysterious.

Take a look at these phrases:

> the rain **fell** in torrents
>
> the sunlight **streamed** through the window, **warming** the tiled floor
>
> crashing thunder **shook** the earth like a giant bellowing in the sky

They all tell you more about the weather than just saying what it is. A good way to say more is to use a verb to show what the weather was doing. Look at the verbs highlighted in blue.

You can also use a simile. This compares the weather to something using 'like' or 'as'. Look at the part highlighted in yellow.

26 Copy and complete these sentences that describe the weather. Start by adding a verb:

(a) The strong wind ...

(d) The cold air ...

(b) The heat of the sun ...

(e) The white clouds ...

(c) Shards of lightning ...

27 Copy and complete these similes about the weather. Make sure you compare the weather to something that really reminds you of it:

(a) The hailstones fell like ...

(d) The wind blew loudly like ...

(b) The mist filled the air like ...

(e) The waves crashed like ...

(c) The sun was as ... as ...

Writing

In this section you will learn how to describe something in great detail. You may sometimes be asked to do this as a task but it is also useful when you are writing stories because you need to describe the setting when you start a story.

There are a number of things you can include in your writing to make it more descriptive:

- Use plenty of adjectives (describing words). Choose ones specific to the place you are describing.
- Use expanded noun phrases.
- Use similes.
- Choose verbs carefully to help build a picture for the reader.
- Use all of your senses, particularly sight, smell and sound.

When you plan your description, think about mood and atmosphere. Depending on what you want the setting to be like, choose the weather conditions carefully:

- Spooky: dark, misty, quiet
- Happy: bright, warm, sunny

- Frightening: dark, cold, shadowy, stormy
- Lonely: quiet, rainy.

Also think about the place you choose to describe:

- Spooky: graveyard, old house, attic, basement
- Happy: beach, park, garden
- Frightening: forest, old church, haunted house
- Lonely: island, desert, mountain top.

The best way to write a description is in the third person and in the past tense. You can change this if you choose but it is a good starting place. Here is an example:

> Standing uncertainly on the street, Number 32 lived up to its reputation as a haunted house. Through the mist, the outline of a ramshackle structure could be seen. The walls were smothered in wilting ivy and the windows were greasy and cracked. Dying bushes and trees littered the front garden and the paving slabs looked like broken teeth, sharp and dangerous. As the front door creaked open, a cloud of dusty cobwebs was dislodged.

Now try these tasks, using the advice you have been given above. Think about a description you have read recently and try to borrow some of the ideas for your own writing.

28 Write a description of a haunted house.

29 Write two short descriptions of the same place, one set during the day and one set at night time.

30 Write a description of a cold, snowy place.

31 Write a description of the most beautiful place you have ever been to.

Hidden hideaways

Can you imagine finding yourself on a remote and exotic island, ready for adventure? Many books have been written about exploring a new land, meeting new people and discovering new creatures. When you read stories of island adventures in this chapter, think about the exploits you might like to create for your own characters as part of their island adventures.

Skill focus: Inference

In this chapter you will practise answering questions that require a little more thinking. You will find clues in the text but, to answer the question, you will have to use what you have read in the text to come up with the answer yourself.

A reading list of stories set in exotic and unusual locations, islands and hidden places, as well as non-fiction books about beautiful parts of the world, can be found in *English Year 4 Answers*.

➔ Comprehension

Making inferences means working out the deeper meaning of a text by 'reading between the lines'. This means you have to put together the clues you have read to understand the text better. Often you will need to make inferences about characters: their feelings, their thoughts and their reasons for doing things. When you are reading for pleasure, you do this all the time, sometimes without even noticing! You also do it with your friends and family, noticing their expressions and behaviour and using that information to infer how they are feeling.

You will need to do a number of things to answer inference questions:

- Look for clues in the text:
  - What do the characters do and say? How do they act and speak?
  - What are they holding, wearing or using?
  - Where are they? Why might they be there?
- Think about what you associate with the words used in the text:
  - Is the language associated with a particular feeling or emotion?
- Use your own experience of the world:
  - Have you ever been in a similar situation?
  - Can you imagine being in that situation?
  - Do you know or have you read about someone in that situation?

Have a look at this example:

Ben's legs were aching. It felt like he had been running for days. Up and down the aisles, past the fridges and freezers, the mountains of fruit and vegetables. Dodging speeding trolleys and busy shoppers. He'd only looked away for a moment. He couldn't resist the draw of the sweets. Millions of them. A tower of sweets in front of him: caramels, fudge, marshmallows, jelly beans. It was like a dream! But when he woke from his dream, he was alone. His mum had gone and he was lost. He looked every which way, his breathing quickened and he tried to call out for his mum but the words would not come. He frantically began running through the maze of shelves. They were crowded with people but to his disappointment, none of them were his mum.

1 Where does this scene take place? How do you know? (2 marks)

The text doesn't actually say where the scene takes place, but there are lots of clues. Find the clues and think about what they remind you of. Some clues are highlighted in yellow for you and your answer might look like this: This passage takes place in a supermarket. (1 mark) I know this because it says, 'dodging speeding trolleys'. (1 mark)

2 How do you think Ben feels in this passage? Refer to the text in your answer. (2 marks)

Look for clues showing how Ben acts to help you. Does this match up with how you would feel in this situation? Some ideas are highlighted in blue.

3 What do you think Ben should do next? Explain your answer fully. (2 marks)

For this question you need to put yourself in the same position as Ben. What would you do that he hasn't already done? The question is worth 2 marks, so remember to say what you think Ben should do next and explain why you think he should do this.

> Now try to answer questions 2 and 3 yourself.

Try this comprehension exercise, using the simple steps above to help you answer the questions. Inference questions are in bold.

Lost in paradise

Michael and his dog Stella have been washed up on a deserted island after falling overboard from their boat. Having looked for help and food unsuccessfully, Michael has decided to build a fire to make a smoke signal he hopes passing boats will see. Suddenly, he catches sight of a man coming out of the undergrowth.

He was diminutive, no taller than me, and as old a man as I had ever seen. He wore nothing but a pair of tattered breeches bunched at the waist, and there was a large knife in his belt. He was thin, too. In places – under his arms, round his neck and his midriff – his copper brown skin lay in folds about him, almost as if he'd shrunk inside
5 it. What little hair he had on his head and his chin was long and wispy and white.

I could see at once that he was very agitated, his chin trembling, his heavily hooded eyes accusing and angry, '*Dameda! Dameda!*' he screeched at me. His whole body was shaking with fury. I backed away as he scuttled up the beach towards me, gesticulating wildly with his stick, and haranguing me as he came. Ancient and
10 skeletal he may have been, but he was moving fast, running almost. '*Dameda! Dameda!*' I had no idea what he was saying. It sounded Chinese or Japanese, maybe.

I was about to turn and run when Stella, who, strangely, had not barked at him at all, suddenly left my side and went bounding off towards him. Her hackles were not up. She was not growling. To my astonishment she greeted him like a long lost friend.

15 He was no more than a few feet away from me when he stopped. We stood looking at each other in silence for a few moments. He was leaning on his stick, trying to catch his breath. 'Americajin? Americajin? American? *Eikokujin?* British?'

'Yes,' I said, relieved to have understood something at last. 'English, I'm English.'

It seemed a struggle for him to get the words out. 'No good. Fire, no good. You
20 understand? No fire,' He seemed less angry now.

'But my mother, my father they might see it, see the smoke.' It was plain he didn't understand me. So I pointed out to sea, by way of explanation. 'Out there. They're out there. They'll see the fire. They'll come and fetch me.'

From *Kensuke's Kingdom* by Michael Morpurgo

---

4 **What can you tell about the old man from the way he looks? (2 marks)**

5 Find two words or phrases that describe how old the man looks.
   (2 marks)

6 **What might have made the old man seem scary? (2 marks)**

7 **What might have reassured the narrator that he didn't need to be scared? (2 marks)**

8 **What do you think 'dameda' means? (1 mark)**

9 **Why do you think it was a 'struggle for him to get the words out' (line 19)? (2 marks)**

Speaking and listening

10 It's time to play an adjectives word game. Sit in a circle. The first person thinks of an adjective. The next person has to think of an adjective that begins with the last letter of the first adjective. For example: funny – yellow – wet. Continue around the circle.

Now try the following comprehension exercise. It is from a different book, but the skills you use are the same.

Relief of rain

Not everybody likes the rain, but for Phillip and Timothy, alone on an island, a heavy rain shower is a welcome surprise. Phillip is the narrator in this story.

During our seventh night on the island, it rained. It was one of those tropical storms that come up swiftly without warning. We were asleep on the palm mats that I'd made, but it awakened us immediately. The rain sounded like bullets hitting on the dried palm frond roof. We ran about in it, shouting and letting the fresh water hit
5 our bodies. It was cool and felt good.

Timothy yelled that his catchment was working. He had taken more boards from the top of the raft and had made a large trough that would catch the rain. He'd picked up bamboo lengths on the beach and had fitted them together into a short pipe to funnel the rain water into out ten-gallon keg.

10 It rained for almost two hours, and Timothy was quite angry with himself for not making a second catchment because the keg was soon filled and overflowing.

We stayed out in the cool rain for twenty or thirty minutes and then went back inside. The roof leaked badly but we didn't mind. We got on our mats and opened our mouths to the sweet, fresh water. Stew Cat was huddled in a miserable ball over
15 in a corner, Timothy said, not enjoying it at all.

I liked the rain because it was something I could hear and feel; not something I must see. It peppered in bursts against the frond roof, and I could hear the drips as it leaked through. The squall wind was in the tops of the palms and I could imagine how they looked in the night sky, thrashing against each other high over our little cay[1].

20 I wanted it to rain all night.

From *The Cay* by Theodore Taylor

[1]cay = a low bank of rock or sand

11 Why do you think the characters are on the island? Give a reason for your answer. (2 marks)

12 What do you think the weather is usually like on the island? Give a reason for your answer. (2 marks)

13 Find three pieces of evidence that show whether Timothy and Phillip enjoyed the rain or not. (3 marks)

14 What is Timothy's 'catchment' (line 6) for and was it successful?
(3 marks)

15 Phillip has a disability. What is it? Refer to the text in your answer.
(2 marks)

Speaking and listening

16 Imagine you are about to be left alone on a desert island. You are allowed to take three luxuries with you. What will you take, and why? Take turns to share your thoughts in discussion groups or pairs and give reasons for your choices.

→ Grammar

In this section you will learn to use fronted adverbials to add extra information to the beginning of your sentences.

Fronted adverbials

A fronted adverbial is a word, or a group of words, at the beginning of a sentence that tells you where, when or how the rest of the sentence happened. It links to the verb in the sentence. Here are some examples:

How?	When?	Where?
Painfully	At sunset	At the end of the road
Bravely	All of a sudden	On the riverbank
With a smile	The day before yesterday	Deep under the sea
Without a sound	Twelve years ago	In the attic
Nervously	As the clock struck eight	Beside the hedge

17 Decide whether these adverbials tell you **when**, **where** or **how**.

(a) Loudly

(b) As the alarm sounded

(c) With great care

(d) Easily

(e) Behind the door

(f) On the other side of the window

(g) At the top of the stairs

(h) Under the bed

(i) Half an hour earlier

(j) Yesterday

18 Write three different fronted adverbials for each of these sentences. One should tell the reader when it happened, one where it happened and one how it happened.

(a) ... the girl jumped into the water.

(b) ... the boat disappeared over the horizon.

(c) ... the birds began to tweet.

➔ Punctuation

In this section, you will learn how to punctuate for fronted adverbials.

Commas for fronted adverbials

In order to make your writing more interesting you can use fronted adverbials to start your sentences. You have already learnt that a fronted adverbial is a word, or a group of words, at the start of a sentence which explains how, when or where the next part of the sentence happened. For example:

Where: At the top of the mountain

When: Ten minutes later

How: With great difficulty

When you use a fronted adverbial to start a sentence, you have to separate it from the rest of the sentence with a comma. For example:

At the top of the mountain, we found the abandoned cottage.

Ten minutes later, the next boat arrived.

With great difficulty, she clambered into the yacht.

19 Copy these sentences and add in the missing commas:

(a) After the storm the sailors breathed a sigh of relief.

(b) On the beach the stranded boys built a shelter.

(c) Quickly and quietly the men ran along the riverbank.

(d) With tears in his eyes the lost boy searched for his friends.

(e) During the storm the boat almost capsized.

20 Match up the fronted adverbial with the rest of the sentence, and copy it out accurately with a comma in the right place.

Fronted adverbial	Rest of the sentence
After hours of digging	the captain carefully steered the boat.
When the wind grew stronger	I crawled out of the water onto the sand.
In an instant	everyone sheltered under the trees.
Past the dangerous rocks	the children found the treasure.
Shaking with cold	a flash of lightning struck the ship's mast.

➲ Spelling

In this chapter you will learn more about homophones. Homophones are words that sound the same but are spelled differently. Here are three of the most commonly confused homophones:

- there: in that place / their: belonging to them / they're: short for 'they are'

- your: belongs to you / you're: short for 'you are'

- to: towards something or in its direction / too: an excess of something; for example, too much / two: the number 2

Here are some other homophones you should know:

- accept: to take something or agree to something / except: apart from
- effect: the result of something / affect: to impact or change something
- peace: calm and quiet / piece: a slice or part of something
- rain: a type of wet weather / rein: used to control a horse / reign: to rule as king or queen
- whose: who does it belong to / who's: short for 'who is'

---

21 Copy these sentences, choosing the right homophone:

(a) There is a lot of rein/reign/rain in tropical countries.

(b) I found a hat but I didn't know whose/who's it was.

(c) The island was beautiful accept/except for the muddy swamps.

(d) The sailors tied up they're/their/there boats by the shore.

(e) If you're/your able to visit a tropical island, don't forget you're/your camera.

22 Match up the homophones from the list below. Look up the words in a dictionary and write a definition for each one.

medal	break
great	mist
ball	meddle
brake	fair
missed	grate
fare	bawl

➔ Vocabulary

When you are writing stories, it is important to think about where your story is set. As the writer, you have a huge amount of choice about the setting. The list is endless, but ideas include:

mountains	beach	island	busy city	farm	forest
hotel	school	park	clifftop	zoo	museum

Even when you are continuing a story, and you already know what the setting is, you need to think of your own ways to describe it without repeating the vocabulary used by the original author.

Once you have chosen your setting, you need to think of words to describe it. These might be:

- nouns: things that you can see, touch, hear, smell or taste in the setting

- adjectives: words to describe the things that you can see, touch, hear, smell and taste in the setting.

Here is an example:

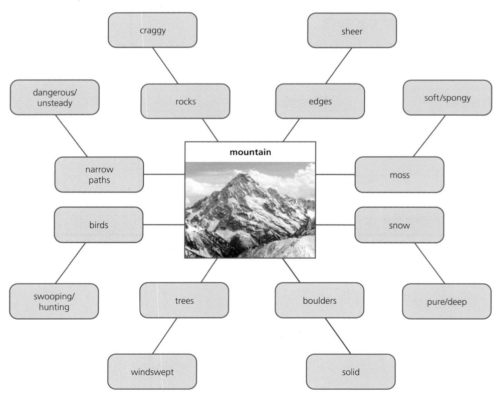

23 Take these three setting ideas: an empty house, a tropical beach in the rain and a deserted island. For each setting, create a spider diagram like the one on the opposite page. Try to find new words that you haven't used before. You could ask a friend, an adult or use a thesaurus to help you.

➲ Writing

In this section, you will learn how to continue a story that you have read.

When you continue a story, it is important that your writing sounds as if the original author wrote it. To do this, you need to look for clues and information in the text and then follow the original author's lead.

- Is the story in the first person (I, we) or the third person (he, she, it, they)?
- Is it in the past tense (he was, he went) or the present tense (he is, he goes)?
- Who are the characters and what are they like?
- Where is the story set and what is it like?
- What mood does the story have? Is it sad, hopeful, mysterious, frightening?

And the most important question:

- What is likely to happen next?
- You will use your inference skills (which you have just practised) to decide what is likely to happen next. Has anything happened already that suggests what's going to happen next? Imagine you were in the story: what would you do next?

Have a look at this example:

One character who is a young person | Slightly mysterious or frightening mood | Third person and past tense

Finally Eve was alone in the house. Although she had spent the whole day feeling desperate for some peace and quiet, now it felt a bit too quiet. The sun had set an hour before and the shadows in the kitchen seemed eerie without the comfort of having her mum or dad in the house. Every creak and squeak that she heard made her shudder. 'Pull yourself together, Eve!' she said aloud to nobody in particular. She checked the front door was locked and stomped upstairs to get on with her homework.

As she sat down and opened her maths book, she heard a door slam downstairs. 'I'm up here, Mum. What did you forget?' she called down the stairs. But nobody replied.

Set in her house | Clues about what might happen next

What would you do if you were Eve? How would you feel? Here are some ideas:

● She goes downstairs and it was a family pet or the wind blowing a door closed.

● She goes downstairs and it was her parents playing a trick on her. Perhaps it is Halloween?

● Perhaps there is someone unexpected in the house: an intruder or another family member?

When you are asked to continue a story, you only need to write a couple of paragraphs. You do not need to finish the whole story, just write the next part.

Now have a go at these tasks by yourself.

24 Continue the story you have just read in the example above. Aim to write two or three more paragraphs.

25 Continue the story about Michael, Stella and the mysterious man that you read on pages 15–16. Aim to write two or three more paragraphs.

26 Continue the story about Phillip and Timothy on the island (page 17). Aim to write two or three more paragraphs.

Dahl directs

Not everything we read is a story. There are many other interesting types of text that we can enjoy. In this chapter you will find out more about the wonderful author Roald Dahl by reading about his life in an autobiography and you'll see how his characters were brought to life on the stage with a play script. Perhaps this will inspire you to write your own play or autobiography.

> ## Skill focus: Purpose and structure
> **In this chapter you will think about the features of different types of texts and how they help the reader to understand and navigate the text better.**

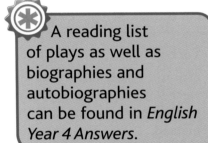
A reading list of plays as well as biographies and autobiographies can be found in *English Year 4 Answers*.

→ Comprehension

As you have looked at several stories already, this chapter will focus on two different types of text: scripts and biographies. When you are reading these types of texts, think about how they are laid out on the page, the language that is used and how they are organised. All of these features are included for a reason.

Scripts

- Scripts are written for actors and directors.
- They show the reader how to perform and stage a play.
- Special features include:
  - clearly marked character names
  - words to be spoken written next to the character name
  - stage directions in brackets.

Biographies and autobiographies

- Biographies and autobiographies are written to tell the reader about a well-known person's life.

- They recount facts about that person and events in their life.

- Special features include:
  - facts, such as names, dates and places
  - descriptions of important events and major achievements
  - that they are written in time order, starting from childhood.

- Biographies are written by somebody other than the subject of the book. Autobiographies are written by the person who is the subject of the book.

Take a look at this example:

Early life

Malorie Blackman was born on 8th February 1962 in London. Her parents were both from Barbados. When she was at school, she wanted to be an English teacher but ended up studying computers and became a systems programmer instead.

Personal life

Malorie married her husband, Neil, in the 1990s and their daughter, Elizabeth, was born in 1995. They now live in Kent. In addition to writing novels, Blackman enjoys playing the piano, computer games and writing poetry.

Work life

Malorie Blackman's first book was published in 1990 and was a collection of short stories called *Not So Stupid*. Since then, she has written another 60 books for children, including novels, short stories, TV scripts and a play. She was won 15 awards for her work and her books have been translated into more than 15 languages.

---

1 What kind of text is this? (1 mark)

Look for clues in the passage. Some have been highlighted for you. How is it written? What is it about? How is it organised? Your answer might look like this:
This is a biography. (1 mark)

2 What is the purpose of the subheadings in this text? (1 mark)

Think about what the subheadings tell you about each paragraph. How do they help the reader?

3 Did Malorie Blackman write this text herself? How do you know? (2 marks)

Look at the language used and think about whose voice is giving the information in this passage.

Now try to answer questions 2 and 3 by yourself.

Try this comprehension exercise, using the guidance above to help you answer the questions. Questions about the purpose and structure of the text are in bold.

Roald Dahl's days

In this passage you will learn more about the famous children's author, Roald Dahl.

Born in Llandaff, Wales, on 13th September 1916 to Norwegian parents, Dahl was named after Roald Amundsen, the Norwegian who had been the first man to reach the South Pole just four years earlier. A heroic start in life.

5 Wanting the best for her only son, his mother sent him to boarding school – first to St Peter's, Weston-super-Mare; then, in 1929, to Repton – where many bizarre and memorable events would later be recounted in *Boy*. Pupils at Repton were invited to trial chocolate bars, a memory that stayed with Dahl throughout his life, inspiring *Charlie and the Chocolate Factory*.

Schooldays happily behind him, Dahl's lust for travel took him first to Canada, then
10 to East Africa, where he worked for an oil company until the outbreak of World War Two. He enlisted in the Royal Air Force at 23 years old.

In September 1940, Dahl received severe injuries to his head, nose and back when his Gladiator crash-landed in the Western Desert. After six months recovering from his injuries in Alexandria he returned to action, taking part in The Battle of Athens.

15 In 1953 Roald Dahl married the American actress, Patricia Neal, with whom he had five children. They divorced after 30 years, and he later married Felicity 'Liccy' Crosland, who has furthered Roald's legacy through the foundation of Roald Dahl's Marvellous Children's Charity and The Roald Dahl Museum and Story Centre.

20 In 1961 *James and the Giant Peach* was published in the US, followed by *Charlie and the Chocolate Factory*. Roald then wrote screenplays for the James Bond hit *You Only Live Twice* and *Chitty Chitty Bang Bang*, as well as adult novels such as *Kiss Kiss*. *Fantastic Mr Fox* was published in 1970, the year before the film *Willy Wonka and the Chocolate Factory* was released. The rest of the decade saw the publication

25 of many other classics, including *Danny the Champion of the World*, *The Enormous Crocodile*, and *My Uncle Oswald*.

Roald also enjoyed enormous success on television. Having already had his stories told in six episodes of the award winning US series *Alfred Hitchcock Presents*, his *Tales of the Unexpected* ran for several series between 1979 and 1988 in the UK.

30 In the early 1980s he published *The Twits*, *Revolting Rhymes*, *The BFG* and *The Witches*. There followed two autobiographical books: *Boy*, in 1984 and *Going*

35 *Solo*, in 1986. *Matilda* was published in 1988, *Esio Trot* in 1990, and finally, in 1991, came the posthumous delight of *The Minpins*.

40 Roald Dahl died on 23 November 1990, aged 74. He was buried in the parish church of St Peter and St Paul in Great Missenden – the

45 Buckinghamshire village where today The Roald Dahl Museum and Story Centre continues his extraordinary mission to amaze, thrill and inspire generations of children and their parents.

Slightly adapted from www.roalddahl.com

4   **What type of text is this? How do you know? (2 marks)**

5   Where did Roald Dahl's name come from? (1 mark)

6   **Why has the author included many dates in the text? (1 mark)**

7   (a) **What are the words in italics? (1 mark)**

   (b) **Why do you think the author has used italics for these words? (1 mark)**

8   **Who do you think would be likely to read this text? (1 mark)**

9   What was unusual about the publication of *The Minpins*? (1 mark)

10 (a) **What are the first and last things this text tells you about Roald Dahl? (2 marks)**

   (b) **Why do you think the text is presented in this order? (1 mark)**

Speaking and listening

11 Imagine you have the chance to interview your favourite author. What questions would you like to ask him or her? Act out the interview, with another person playing the role of the author and imagining his or her answers. You could do some research about the author first, to help you ask the best questions. There is usually a short biography of the author at the beginning or end of books.

Now try this comprehension exercise. It is based on a script, which has many specific features to make it clear and useful for the reader.

Inside the giant peach

James has discovered an enormous peach and has finally found a way inside. But what will he find?

(James discovers a hole in the side of the giant peach, and bravely enters.)

	Old-green-grasshopper:	Look who's here!
	Centipede:	We've been waiting for you!
	James:	Oh no! No! (James acts scared to death and frozen with fear
5		as the curtain opens slowly to reveal Old-green-grasshopper, Spider, Ladybird, Centipede, and Earthworm sitting comfortably. Silkworm is curled up asleep in a corner)
	Spider:	I'm hungry!
	Old-green-grasshopper:	I'm famished!
10	Ladybird:	So am I!
	Centipede:	Everyone's famished! We need food!

(Pause, as all look at James)

Spider: (Leaning toward James) Aren't you hungry?

(James is still petrified with fear)

15 Old-green-grasshopper: (To James) What's the matter with you? You look positively ill!

Centipede: He looks as though he's going to faint any second.

Ladybird: Oh, my goodness, the poor thing! I do believe he thinks it's *him* we are wanting to eat!

(Everyone roars with laughter)

20 All: Oh dear, oh dear! What an awful thought!

Ladybird: You mustn't be frightened. We wouldn't *dream* of hurting you. You are one of us now, didn't you know that? You are one of the crew. We're all in the same boat.

Old-green-grasshopper: We've been waiting for you all day long. We thought you
25   were never going to turn up. I'm glad you made it.

Centipede: So, cheer up, my boy, cheer up! And meanwhile I wish you'd come over here and give me a hand with these boots. It takes me hours to get them all off by myself.

(James crosses the room and kneels beside Centipede)

30   Thank you so much. You are very kind.

James:	Well … uh … you have a lot of boots.
Centipede:	I have a lot of legs and a lot of feet. One hundred, to be exact. (Proudly) I *am* a centipede, you know.
Earthworm:	*There* he goes again! He simply cannot stop telling lies about his legs! He's only got forty-two! The trouble is that most people don't bother to count them. And anyway, there is nothing *marvellous*, you know, Centipede, about having a lot of legs.
Centipede:	Poor Earthworm. (Whispering in James's ear) He's blind, you know. He can't see how splendid I look.
Earthworm:	In my opinion, the *really* marvellous thing is to have no legs at all and to be able to walk just the same.
Centipede:	You call that *walking*! You're a *slitherer*, that's all you are! You just *slither* along.
Earthworm:	I *glide*.
Centipede:	You are a slimy beast.
Earthworm:	I am *not* a slimy beast. I am a useful and much-loved creature. Ask any gardener you like. And as for you …
Centipede:	I am a *pest*! (Grinning proudly and looking round the room for approval)
Ladybird:	He is *so* proud of that, though for the life of me I cannot understand why. Oh … please excuse me … my name is Ladybird.

Lines: 35, 40, 45, 50

From Roald Dahl's *James and the Giant Peach*, dramatised by Richard George

12 Who is the first character to speak in this extract? (1 mark)

13 (a) How does James feel when he first enters the peach? (1 mark)

(b) How do you know that James feels that way? (1 mark)

14 When James speaks, how does the playwright show that he is scared? (2 marks)

15 Why do you think some words are in italics? (1 mark)

16 What is the purpose of the words in brackets? (1 mark)

17 Does the centipede mind being a pest? How do you know? (2 marks)

18 What action might the actor playing Ladybird do as he speaks his final line? (1 mark)

19 Divide into groups of about three or four. Then read the passage from *James and the Giant Peach* together, taking a character each and doubling up if you need to. As you read the script aloud, take special notice of the exclamation marks, and use lots of expression whenever you see one.

➔ Grammar

In this section you will learn to use adverbs. They are very useful when writing stage directions.

Adverbs

Adverbs are words that describe verbs (doing words). They tell you more about a verb.

Many adverbs end in -ly. You make the adverb by adding -ly to the adjective (a describing word). For example:

> quick + ly ⟶ She ran **quickly**.
> sudden + ly ⟶ He appeared **suddenly**.
> brave + ly ⟶ They fought **bravely**.

Usually, you don't have to change the adjective at all; you just add -ly. For example:

> careful + ly ⟶ He worked **carefully**.
> truthful + ly ⟶ We spoke **truthfully**.

However, there are some exceptions, which you will learn in the spelling section on page 34.

---

20 Add -ly to these adjectives to make adverbs.

(a) bright	**(e)** final	**(i)** usual
(b) loud	**(f)** painful	**(j)** complete
(c) clear	**(g)** successful	**(k)** definite
(d) kind	**(h)** powerful	**(l)** absolute

21 Now write a sentence for each of the adverbs you have made above.

➔ Punctuation

When you are writing a playscript, you need to use punctuation slightly differently from they way you do in other types of writing.

Punctuating a script

In a play, all of the words are spoken out loud so speech marks aren't used. The sentences spoken by the actors are punctuated as usual. Brackets are used around words that shouldn't be spoken, such as stage directions. For example:

Character names show
who is speaking

No speech marks
are needed

Centipede: He looks as though he's going to faint any second.

Ladybird: Oh, my goodness, the poor thing! I do believe he thinks it's *him* we are wanting to eat!

(Everyone roars with laughter)

Stage directions are in brackets
so that the actors know not to say
them aloud.

Normal sentence
punctuation

22 Turn this piece of text into script, using the layout and punctuation you have seen above:

As the clock struck eight, Kim-Hu walked into the kitchen.

'Good morning,' whispered Kim-Hu, yawning.

'You're finally awake,' replied his mother. 'I thought you'd never be ready for school in time.'

Kim-Hu sat down at the table and began to eat the breakfast his mum had made for him.

'You always say that, Mum, but I've never actually been late,' he said, loudly munching his toast as his mum walked out of the kitchen in a hurry, muttering under her breath.

➔ Spelling

As you have already learnt, many adverbs are made by adding the suffix -ly to an adjective. However, sometimes you have to change the spelling of the adjective before you add the suffix.

If the adjective ends in a -y, change it to an -i before adding -ly. For example:

easy + ly ——➤ They won **easily**.

If the adjective ends in -le, just change -le to -ly. For example:

gentle + ly ——➤ They stirred the soup **gently**.

If the adjective ends in -ic, add -ally instead of -ly. For example:

basic + ally ——➤ They were **basically** the same.

There are also a few total exceptions to these rules:

true ——➤ truly   due ——➤ duly   public ——➤ publicly   whole ——➤ wholly

---

23 Turn these adjectives into adverbs by adding -ly. Be careful with the spelling.

(a) simple	**(f)** happy
(b) noble	**(g)** possible
(c) humble	**(h)** busy
(d) dramatic	**(i)** angry
(e) frantic	**(j)** terrible

24 Now write a sentence using each of the adverbs you have made above.

➔ Vocabulary

In this chapter, you have thought about characters speaking in plays. In plays, stage directions tell the actors how to say the words and what to do. You can't use stage directions in stories, but you can use the following pattern to give the reader more information about how the character is speaking:

What he said + how he said it + what he did when he said it.

For example:

'Ouch!' said Danny.

becomes

'Ouch!' cried Danny suddenly, grabbing his stomach with his right hand.

Marie said, 'Are we nearly home, Mummy?'

becomes

Shaking with cold, Marie softly whispered, 'Are we nearly home, Mummy?'

Notice that for the 'how he said it' part, you can use an interesting word for 'said' and an adverb (a describing word that tells you more about the verb).

---

25 Use a thesaurus to help you make these sentences more interesting by adding extra words, as in the examples above.

(a) 'Where are we?' said my brother.

(b) Jenny said, 'I'm tired.'

(c) 'I asked you to be quiet,' said Mr Holmes.

(d) 'I passed my exam,' said Milly.

(e) Sita said, 'Wow! It's amazing.'

➔ Writing

In this chapter, you have seen a script. Now it is your turn to write one. Remember the features that you saw earlier:

- character names on the left
- words spoken by the characters next to their names
- no speech marks
- stage directions in brackets

There are different types of stage directions. Try to include all of them:

- Setting the scene: these help the people putting on the play, designing the scenery and finding and making the props.

- Entering and exiting: these tell the actors when and where to go on and off the stage.

- Actions: these describe the actions that the actors need to do. They tell them how to move around the stage, where to stand and what to do.

- Speaking: these are given just before a line of text and tell the actor how to say the words. They might say how loud the line should be spoken or they might indicate that the line should be said with a particular emotion.

- Sound effects and lighting: these give instructions about when lights go on and off or when parts of the stage go darker or lighter, or about the sound effects or music being played to add to the mood.

Now have a go at these tasks using the advice above to help you. Have a look at the extract from *James and the Giant Peach* to help you set out your script correctly on the page.

26 Write a short play about two characters meeting for the first time.

27 Write a play that retells a story, or part of a story, that you already know well.

28 Write a scene from a play in which night falls during the scene. Include information about lighting in your stage directions to show day turning into night.

29 Choose one of the characters from *James and the Giant Peach* and create your own play with that character in it.

 **Dino discoveries**

Dinosaurs have been the topic of thousands of books, poems, films and documentaries. Why are they so fascinating? Perhaps because they are so different from modern creatures? They lived such a long time ago that there will always be a sense of mystery about how they lived, looked and ultimately disappeared. This element of the unknown provides food for the imagination for both readers and writers.

Skill focus: Author's use of language

In this chapter, you are going to learn how to explain why authors use particular words and phrases in their writing. Thinking about how published writers use words and phrases also helps you improve your own writing, because you can borrow some of their ideas.

A reading list of fiction and non-fiction books about dinosaurs can be found in *English Year 4 Answers*.

→ Comprehension

When an author is writing, they choose their words very carefully to help the reader grasp an idea, see a picture in their head or feel a feeling. They might use:

- well-chosen adjectives
- verbs that tell you more about the action
- **similes**: these are phrases that compare two things using the words 'like' or 'as'. For example:

The plane soared through the night sky like a shooting star.

- **metaphors**: these are phrases that describe one thing as if it were another. For example:

  The fence had iron teeth, keeping people away.

- **personification**: this is when something non-human is described as if it is human and is displaying human emotions or actions. For example:

  The gentle breeze tickled my skin.

If you are asked about why the author has used these different language techniques, you can do a number of things to help you answer the question:

- Close your eyes and think about what you see when you bring the words to mind.

- Look at the words one by one and work out what you associate with them.

- Think about what is being described and what you already know about it.

- Imagine you are the writer. Why would you choose that particular word rather than another? What in particular does it tell you?

Have a look at this example:

The verb 'gripped' is used.

The car is compared to a rollercoaster. This is a simile.

The rain is compared to tears. This is another simile.

They were late. Dad put his foot down and the car sped over the hills like a rollercoaster ride. Annie gripped the seat tightly, her knuckles turning white. Being late wasn't the only disappointment of the day. The weather was changing. Raindrops were running down the car windows like tears and the threatening grey clouds stared at them from above. Suddenly Annie saw a flash of lightning and soon the thunder began to bellow angrily. There was a battle in the sky.

The thunder is given an emotion: anger. This is also personification.

There is not really a battle. The word 'battle' is used to represent the bad weather. This is a metaphor.

The clouds are described as staring. They cannot really stare, because they have no eyes. This is personification.

1 (a) What does the author compare the car to? (1 mark)

(b) What does that tell you about the car? (1 mark)

Scan for the word 'car' and reread the part in green. Now think about a rollercoaster. What are they like? How do they move? How is that like a car going over hills? Your answer might look like this:

(a) The car is compared to a rollercoaster. (1 mark)

(b) It shows how the car is going up and down over hills like a rollercoaster riding up and down the rails. (1 mark)

2 What does the word 'gripped' tell you about the way Annie is feeling? (2 marks)

Think about what it means to grip something. It means Annie is holding on much more tightly than normal. Why would she be holding on so tightly?

3 (a) What does the author mean by 'a battle in the sky'? (1 mark)

There clearly isn't actually a battle happening in the sky. What is happening in the sky? Reread the relevant part of the text. Does anything that is happening look or sound like a battle?

(b) What is 'a battle in the sky' an example of? (1 mark)

metaphor   simile   adjective

The phrase doesn't contain an adjective (a describing word) and the phrase doesn't include the words 'like' or 'as'. This narrows it down.

Now try to answer questions 2 and 3 yourself.

Try the following comprehension exercise, using the guidance above to help you answer the questions. Questions about the author's use of language are in bold.

A surprising find

Jessica and her friends are exploring the cliffs and caves where the river meets the sea at Clademouth. They know they shouldn't have come this far alone, and are just about to head back, when they make a very unusual discovery …

'Look,' said Jessica, 'I think we ought to go back. We'll get into awful trouble if anything happens to Tim.'

'That's just an excuse,' said Tim. 'You're just frightened like the rest of us.'

'All right, I am frightened,' said Jessica. 'All this earth slid about during the night, and
5 who's to say it won't go on sliding about and trap us underneath it. This whole lot could shift at any minute. It's too dangerous here.'

And shift it did. As Jessica spoke, the ground they sat on rippled and flexed, and the slope they had slid down reared up and twisted. The slope was a neck. Fergus ran the light of the torch up it, and found a small pointed head. As the terrified children
10 watched, two yellow eyes opened and blinked. Fergus dropped the torch which must never be moved from the shelf inside the kitchen door, and the children ran towards the light, stumbling over each other and gasping for breath, their lungs tight with fear. They tumbled out onto the ruins of the cliff, and lay panting in the morning sun. None of them spoke.

15 But something did. From deep in the cavern, with a strange sound like the wind over milk bottles (which the children had never heard, for milk bottles had not been used for years) they heard something singing. It sang one word, over and over again.

'Frightened. Frightened. Frightened.'

'I'm going to see what it is,' said Jessica. 'The rest of you stay here.'

20 'Rubbish! We're all going with you,' said Billy.

'Besides,' said Tim, 'we've got to get the torch back.'

It took some time for their eyes to readjust to the gloom. It took a little more time to realize what it was they were looking at, for the dinosaur nearly filled the cavern, and they could not see right to the far end of her. But the two browny-grey tree trunk
25 legs and the long neck with its pointed, duck-like head (and still those yellow eyes blinking worriedly at them) left them with only one possible conclusion.

'It's a dinosaur.' said Dixie.

From *Brilliant the Dinosaur* by Richard Stilgoe

4 Find and copy three verbs from lines 7–8 that show how the ground moved at the beginning of the passage. (3 marks)

5 Why did the ground move? (2 marks)

6 (a) 'Stumbling over each other and gasping for breath' (line 12): How did the children feel at this point? How do you know? (3 marks)

(b) Find and copy another phrase that shows they felt this way. (1 mark)

7 'a strange sound like the wind over milk bottles' (lines 15–16). What technique has the author used here? (1 mark)

8 (a) What does the author compare the dinosaur's legs to? (1 mark)

(b) What does this tell you about the dinosaur's legs? (1 mark)

Speaking and listening

9 In groups of five, act out the scene from the passage in which the children explore the cliffs by the sea at Clademouth and make their astonishing discovery. Rehearse your scene and then perform it to the rest of the class.

Now try this comprehension exercise. Questions about a writer's use of language can be asked of any text and this is an example of non-fiction. Think about the purpose of the text as you answer the questions.

The long-necked beast

Everyone recognises the long-necked shape of the Diplodocus, but what were they really like?

The Diplodocus was one of the biggest dinosaurs ever to walk the Earth. It belonged to a group of dinosaurs called *sauropods*. It was 26m long and its great weight (15 tons) was supported by huge straight legs, like pillars.

The Diplodocus looked extraordinary with its long neck and tail, and a head that
5 was tiny in proportion to the rest of its body. This type of body suited its lifestyle
perfectly. It could reach up to feed at the tops of the very tall trees, like conifers, that
grew at the time. Its small head allowed it to browse amongst the vegetation, where
few other dinosaurs could reach.

This type of feeding needed a special type of neck – one that was strong, light, and
10 flexible, in order to be raised and lowered easily. Having stripped one area bare
of food, it would have ambled off with its companions in search of new feeding
grounds. If Diplodocus was threatened by a meat eater, its only defence would have
been its bulk, and its long, whip-like tail.

Although Diplodocus is often shown living in marshy land, this habitat would not
15 have suited it at all. Because it had quite narrow feet in proportion to its body weight
(like an elephant's), it probably would have sunk into the mire[1] and got stuck. It
would have preferred a landscape with dry, firm ground, where it would browse its
way through conifer forests, perhaps as part of a herd.

The design of a Diplodocus's neck is rather like that of a man-made crane. The jib,
20 which juts out from the main tower and
from which the hooks used for lifting
are suspended, is like the dinosaur's
neck. The heavy base of the crane
which keeps it from toppling over is
25 like a Diplodocus's sturdy body. The jib
of a crane has to be light and strong,
so the engineer builds it with a light
metal framework. Diplodocus had
lightweight, but very strong, bones in its
30 neck, which it could raise and lower like
the jib of a crane.

From *Eyewitness Guides: Dinosaur* by David
Norman and Angela Milner

[1] mire = area of muddy swamp or bog

10 Which group of dinosaurs does the Diplodocus belong to? (1 mark)

11 (a) What does the author compare the Diplodocus' legs to? (1 mark)

(b) Why is this a good comparison? (1 mark)

12 How did the Diplodocus protect itself from predators? (2 marks)

13 Why would the Diplodocus have preferred a dry landscape to a marshy one? (2 marks)

14 (a) What does the author compare the Diplodocus's neck to in the last paragraph? (1 mark)

(b) Find two ways in which the Diplodocus's neck and the thing it is compared to are similar. (2 marks)

Speaking and listening

15 Choose a dinosaur and prepare a two-minute talk about it to present to the rest of the class. To do this you will need to do some research, using books and the internet. Try to use pictures and diagrams in your talk; audiences generally like something to look at as well as listen to. You will need to think about the dinosaur's name, habitat, diet, size and weight.

➔ Grammar

In this section you will learn how to use pronouns to help your writing flow well.

Pronouns

Pronouns are short words that are used instead of nouns. Using a pronoun stops you from repeating the noun over and over again and helps link sentences together. Pronouns include:

I   me   you   he   she   it   him   her   we   us   they   them

For example:

Amina zoomed down the road on her scooter. **It** was shiny and red and **she** could ride **it** very fast.

The 'it' refers to the scooter and the 'she' refers to Amina. It would sound odd if you didn't use pronouns:

Amina zoomed down the road on her scooter. **Her scooter** was shiny and red and **Amina** could ride **the scooter** very fast.

When you use pronouns, make sure it is clear what the pronoun is replacing. If you use too many pronouns and it isn't clear what they refer to, your writing might become confusing:

Dad and Uncle Tim walked into the kitchen and he picked it up. He passed it to him and he left the room.

In this sentence it's very unclear who is doing what and what has been picked up. There are too many pronouns!

16 Copy these sentences and underline the pronouns:

(a) Billy was very excited when he saw the dinosaur skeleton.

(b) He thought it was the most incredible thing he had ever seen.

(c) Billy's mum asked him what kind of dinosaur it was.

(d) She didn't know much about them but Billy did.

(e) He told her that it was a Diplodocus and that they were one of the tallest dinosaurs.

(f) I went to the museum too, but I preferred to look at the blue whale.

(g) It was even bigger than I had imagined.

(h) We had a wonderful day at the museum and the memory will stay with us for a long time.

17 Copy out this passage, adding in the missing pronouns:

My friend Carmen created a project about dinosaurs. ___ spent a long time researching ___. ___ went to the library by herself and read more than 15 books about ___. At school, everyone was impressed. ___ all hoped she would get to read it out in assembly. The teacher really liked ___ and even displayed ___ in the library. ___ all read it at lunchtime and now ___ go to Carmen when ___ have questions about dinosaurs. ___ is the expert!

➔ Punctuation

If you include the actual words that characters say in your story, this is called direct speech. You must use speech marks to show when characters are talking.

Direct speech

It is important to punctuate direct speech accurately, to help the reader understand who is speaking when. There are several rules to remember:

- Put speech marks around the words that are spoken.

  'I'd like to be an archaeologist to learn about dinosaurs,' stated Ramina.

- The spoken words should begin with a capital letter. The exception to this rule is when the spoken words are interrupted by some narration. In this situation, no capital letter is needed when the spoken words start up again.

  'Some dinosaurs,' commented Charley, 'were over 12 metres tall.'

- Separate the speaking from the narration with a comma.
- Punctuate what is inside the speech marks as usual.

  Dani put down his book and said, 'Wow! Dinosaurs were so scary.'

- When a new person starts speaking, start a new line.

It is also important to remember that when you are writing by hand it is usual to use a pair of speech marks each time: " ". Stories that appear in print, however, often use single speech marks: ' '.

---

18 Copy out the following sentences and add in the missing punctuation:

    (a) please can we go to the museum to see the dinosaur skeletons asked James

    (b) look yelled Mina i think i found a fossil

    (c) Tyrannosaurus Rex is my favourite dinosaur replied Robbie

    (d) some dinosaurs only ate plants declared the tour guide

    (e) if i could travel back in time said Mia i would love to see the dinosaurs

19 Imagine you are talking to an expert about dinosaurs. Write a short conversation. Use speech marks and don't forget the 'new speaker, new line' rule.

➜ Spelling

In English, there are some words that don't follow any particular rules. They are just tricky to spell. Many people spell these words incorrectly so it is important to learn them. A good way to do this is to have a 'spelling voice'. This is a voice in your head that says the words exactly as they are spelled to help you to spell them correctly. For example:

| friend | say out loud 'frend' | say in your head 'fry-end' |
| business | say out loud 'bizniss' | say in your head 'bus-ee-ness' |

20 Think of ways to help you remember these spellings, using your spelling voice.

(a) different   (e) important   (i) purpose

(b) interesting   (f) knowledge   (j) sentence

(c) disappear   (g) medicine   (k) separate

(d) favourite   (h) occasionally   (l) special

21 Now write a series of sentences, using one of these words in each sentence.

➜ Vocabulary

If you are writing about creatures such as dinosaurs, you will need to describe how they move in order to bring them to life. Different words create different pictures in the reader's mind. For example:

A huge, slow dinosaur might **lurch**, **stomp** or **lumber**.

A smaller, faster dinosaur might **sprint**, **scamper** or **scurry**.

You need to match the movement to the type of dinosaur. Scary, dangerous beasts might move in a very different way from friendly, harmless creatures. It is therefore important to know exactly what a range of different verbs mean so that you can choose the right one for your beast.

22 Write a definition for each of the following words. Use a dictionary to help you.

(a) soar   (e) trudge   (i) stalk

(b) scuttle   (f) roam   (j) traipse

(c) dash   (g) trundle

(d) prance   (h) pounce

23 Now write a series of sentences, using one of these words in each sentence. Try to write about dinosaurs or other creatures.

➲ Writing

In this section you are going to write stories about dinosaurs. A good story needs a number of ingredients:

- a well-described setting
- two or three well-described characters
- a problem or a challenge, which the characters have to overcome
- an exciting first sentence or two
- a clear, satisfying ending.

The most important thing about your story is that it is interesting and people want to read on. To help make sure this happens:

- use a range of interesting and varied vocabulary
- use some similes, personification and/or metaphors
- plan carefully so that the main event is exciting and interesting
- don't give too much away too quickly; leave the reader guessing what might happen next
- describe your characters well so that the reader believes in them.

Another good tip is to 'show not tell'. This means showing how characters behave and speak to allow readers to get to know them and work out for themselves what they are like and how they are feeling. For example:

Telling: Trexxy was a strong dinosaur, who was tall and frightening.

Showing: Trexxy towered over the other dinosaurs, his muscly legs causing the ground to vibrate as they stomped on the ground. All the other dinosaurs quivered and cowered when he strode up the mountain.

Telling: The ground was cold and there was a strong wind.

Showing: Her boots crunched on the frozen ground and she wrapped her coat tightly around her to keep out the frosty air.

Although it takes a bit longer and a few more words, showing the reader gives them a much better impression of what is happening. It can help the reader to feel they are part of the story.

24 Write a story set in a dinosaur exhibition at a museum.

25 Write a story in which all of the characters are dinosaurs.

26 Write a story about a fossil. It could be lost or found, real or imaginary, but it should be the focus of the story.

27 Write a story with the title 'The Secret Cave'.

Tales of war

Times of conflict are full of emotion and therefore make a good backdrop for stories. The combination of adventure, danger, excitement, strong feelings and the presence of both good and evil characters interests readers and inspires writers. Stories based on real events are also appealing to readers as they feel sympathy for the characters and wonder what their experiences were really like. Enjoy these war-based texts and draw some ideas from them for your own writing.

Skill focus: Joining the dots
In this chapter you will revise and practise the skills you have already worked on in Chapters 1 to 4.

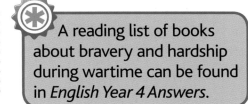
A reading list of books about bravery and hardship during wartime can be found in *English Year 4 Answers*.

➔ Comprehension

In the previous chapters, you have worked on four key skills:

- Retrieval: This involves scanning the whole text for the answers and copying them down.

- Inference: This involves working out what the question is asking, looking for clues in the text and using the clues to form an answer.

- Purpose and structure: This involves thinking about how the layout and features of a text, and the way a text is ordered, help the reader to understand what the text is trying to tell them.

- Author's use of language: This involves thinking about how and why an author chooses particular vocabulary and language techniques, including similes, personification and metaphors.

Try this comprehension exercise. You can also look back at previous chapters to help you if you get stuck.

Together at last

After years of war and a dangerous journey from Poland to the safety of Switzerland, Ruth Balicki is thrilled to find her parents, at last.

It was dark when Ruth opened her eyes. She was being lifted up.

A man's voice said, 'It's a girl – thin as a string of seaweed and wringing wet. How you feeling, eh? We nearly ran you down in the dark.'

He spoke in a strange language which Ruth did not understand. She tried to speak, but no words came.

'She's worrying about something,' said the man.

'Better take her below and get some dry clothes on her,' said someone else.

Her mind drifted to a blank.

When she woke again, she was lying in a bunk. There was a light above her, dry blankets round her, and a flicker of warmth in her limbs.

'Where am I?' she said.

Strange faces peered down at her from the sky. There was a cup at her lips.

'Feed her slowly,' a man was saying. 'Don't give her too much or she'll be sick.'

The cup came back again, and biscuits too. She sat up.

'Edek! Bronia! Jan!' she cried.

'Polish names,' said a woman's voice. 'I said she was Polish. Anyone talk Polish?' And Ruth, frightened by the unfamiliar faces, cried out again, 'Edek! Bronia! Jan!'

And suddenly from the back of the crowd came the echo, 'Edek! Bronia! Jan!' in a deep voice. Dazed and bewildered though she was, she knew it for her father's voice. Now she was gathered in his arms, smothered with his kisses. She tried to speak, to listen to what he was saying. But her head was throbbing and she was too tired to keep her eyes open.

When she woke again, her father's face was close to hers.

'You've been asleep a long time,' he said. 'Try to stay awake and I'll show you what you want to see.'

The blankets pressed round her and she felt herself being lifted from the bunk.

'Look down there,' said Joseph.

30 She saw, in a nest of blankets, Bronia's sleeping head. There was a flush of colour on the child's cheeks and she was snoring.

'Nothing much wrong with her,' said Joseph, and he carried Ruth to the next bunk. She looked again and saw Edek's face. It was very white, and he was lying still and as straight as a post.

'Is he breathing?' she said.

35 'Yes, he's breathing,' said Joseph, 'but only just.' And he carried her quickly away and showed her Jan.

He was sitting on his blankets, dangling his legs over the edge of the bunk. There was a glint of mischief in his eyes.

'They're a feeble lot, the Balickis,' he said. 'They would all have drowned if it hadn't
40 been for me. Ruth, you're crazy. Fancy going for a sail in weather like this – and thinking you could manage without me! You use an oar like a soup spoon, and when a little water comes in the boat you faint. I had to find Edek's boat and steer ours to it. I shouted to him to help, but he'd fainted too. The water was nearly up to his neck. So I pulled him over the side into our boat – two seconds before his turned over and
45 sank.'

Joseph patted his cheek affectionately. 'Eat up your bread and cheese and stop boasting,' he said. 'If you say any more, you'll go off pop.'

Ruth reached out her arms to Jan and gave him a hug. 'You ought to be made an admiral at once,' she said. 'Thank God they're safe, all three of them.' And then she
50 flung her arms round her father's neck.

'You've got your numbers wrong. I haven't finished yet. Hey, don't strangle me!' he said. And he carried her out of the cabin.

'There *are* only three,' said Ruth. 'What do you mean?'

'The last and best surprise,' said Joseph, opening another door. 'I tried to tell you over
55 the phone, but I couldn't make myself heard.'

The cabin was small, and there was only one person in it. She had been waiting for the door to open. Her eyes were wide with expectation, her arms stretched out in welcome.

'Mother!' said Ruth, and with a happiness that no words can describe she slipped
60 from her father's arms into those other arms, so eager to receive her.

From *The Silver Sword* by Ian Serraillier

1 Where is Ruth from? (1 mark)

2 'thin as a string of seaweed' (line 2)

   (a) Which technique has the author used here? (1 mark)

   (b) Why do you think the author chose this comparison for the girl? (2 marks)

3 'Her mind drifted to a blank.' (line 8) What does the author mean by this? (1 mark)

4 What kind of people do you think the strangers in the passage are? Give reasons for your answer. (3 marks)

5 'he was lying still and as straight as a post' (lines 32–33)

   What does this simile tell you about the boy? (2 marks)

6 Find two pieces of evidence that show that Ruth was pleased to see her family again. (2 marks)

7 Why do you think the author has chosen to wait to reveal Ruth's mother until the very end of the passage? (1 mark)

Speaking and listening

8 Read the passage about Ruth and her family again. Then work in a group to put on a short play about what happens in the passage. You can take a role each and act out the scene, beginning with the moment when Ruth wakes up to find herself surrounded by strangers.

Now try the following comprehension exercise. It is based on a letter and will allow you to practise all of the skills you have learnt.

Brave Anne

The story of how brave, thirteen-year old Anne Frank lived in hiding in Amsterdam to escape the Nazis is well known across the world. To keep her spirits up during this difficult time, she kept a diary.

Wednesday 23rd February 1944

Dear Kitty,

It's lovely weather outside and I've quite perked up since yesterday. Nearly every morning I go to the attic where Peter works, to blow the stuffy air out of my lungs.
5　From my favourite spot on the floor I look up at the blue sky and the bare chestnut tree, on whose branches little raindrops glisten like silver, and at the seagulls and other birds as they glide on the wind.

He stood with his head against a thick beam, and I sat down. We breathed the fresh air, looked outside and both felt that the spell should not be broken by words. We
10　remained like this for a long time, and when he had to go up to the loft to chop wood, I knew that he was a nice fellow. He climbed the ladder, and I followed; then he chopped wood for about a quarter of an hour, during which time we still remained silent. I watched him from where I stood; he was obviously doing his best to show off his strength. But I looked out of the open window too, over a large area
15　of Amsterdam, over all the roofs and on to the horizon, which was such a pale blue that it was hard to see the dividing line. 'As long as this exists,' I thought, 'and I may live to see it, this sunshine, the cloudless skies, while this lasts, I cannot be unhappy.'

The best remedy for those who are afraid, lonely or unhappy is to go outside, somewhere they can be quiet, alone with the heavens, nature and God. Because
20　only then does one feel that all is as it should be and that God wishes to see people happy, amidst the simple beauty of nature. As long as this exists, and it certainly always will, I know that then there will always be comfort for every sorrow, whatever the circumstances may be. And I firmly believe that nature brings solace in all
25　troubles.

Oh, who knows, perhaps it won't be long before I can share this overwhelming feeling of bliss with someone who feels the way I do about it.

Yours,

30　*ANNE*

From *The Diary of Anne Frank* by Anne Frank

■ Anne Frank, 1929–45

9 What had cheered Anne up at the start of the letter? (1 mark)

10 Who do you think Kitty is? (1 mark)

11 'raindrops glisten like silver' (line 6)

   (a) What technique has the author used in this phrase? (1 mark)

   (b) Why is the comparison between raindrops and silver a good one to make? (2 marks)

12 What did Anne think of Peter? Refer to the text in your answer. (2 marks)

13 What did Anne believe was the best cure for unhappiness? Explain in your own words. (2 marks)

14 Why is there a date at the top of this text? (2 marks)

15 What kind of person do you think Anne Frank was? Give reasons from the text in your answer. (4 marks)

Speaking and listening

16 In her diary, Anne Frank suggests that 'The best remedy for those who are afraid, lonely or unhappy is to go outside, somewhere they can be quiet, alone with the heavens, nature and God'. Do you agree? How do you cheer yourself up when you are feeling sad? In small discussion groups, share your thoughts.

➲ Grammar

Answer these questions to find out what you remember about expanded noun phrases, fronted adverbials, adverbs and pronouns.

17 Create expanded noun phrases based on these nouns. Include a preposition (a word showing position or direction).

   (a) house   (c) blanket   (e) song

   (b) diary   (d) stranger

18 Use these fronted adverbials to create full sentences:

    (a) Every afternoon,   **(d)** Smiling happily,

    (b) Up in the attic,   **(e)** Late into the evening,

    (c) Without saying a word,

19 Add appropriate adverbs to these sentences. Think carefully about where to place each adverb.

    (a) She climbed to the top of the stairs and looked out of the window.

    (b) She wrote in her diary and placed it under her pillow.

    (c) She drank the tea and ate the bread.

    (d) He found the shed and opened the door.

    (e) She greeted her mother and hugged her.

20 Underline the pronouns in these sentences:

    (a) I asked Mum for my blanket and she passed it to me.

    (b) He was hungry and he wanted the cake so he took it from the cake tin.

    (c) Susie and I enjoyed visiting the war museum and we would like to visit it again.

    (d) They were so glad to see him that they shouted for joy.

    (e) She wasn't sure what to do so she asked them for help.

21 Replace the underlined nouns with an appropriate pronoun:

    (a) Helena took her toothbrush and <u>Helena</u> brushed her teeth with <u>the toothbrush</u>.

    (b) Sam and his brothers boarded the train in London and <u>Sam and his brothers</u> got off <u>the train</u> in Manchester.

    (c) Hadi entered the classroom and picked up a pencil, then <u>Hadi</u> began to write a story with <u>the pencil</u>.

    (d) Mum and I went to the supermarket and <u>Mum and I</u> walked all around <u>the supermarket</u> until we found the milk.

    (e) Carly ran very fast in the race. <u>Carly</u> won the race and <u>Carly</u> received a gold medal.

➔ Punctuation

In this section you will practise basic sentence punctuation, commas for fronted adverbials, punctuating a script and punctuating direct speech.

22 Copy out this passage and add in the missing punctuation. You should end up with four sentences:

anne frank lived in amsterdam during the second world war she had to hide from the nazis because she was jewish she lived in an attic and could never go outside the door to the attic was hidden by a bookcase and she lived there for over two years with her family

23 Copy these sentences and add in the missing commas:

(a) Hiding in the attic Anne Frank was lonely.

(b) Behind the bookcase the door to the attic room was well hidden.

(c) Almost every day Anne Frank wrote in her diary.

(d) Secretly people helped the Frank family to stay safe.

(e) After two years the family was discovered.

24 Turn this passage into a script. Make sure you include all the necessary punctuation:

When she woke again, her father's face was close to hers.

'You've been asleep a long time,' he said. 'Try to stay awake and I'll show you what you want to see.'

'Look down there. Nothing much wrong with her,' said Joseph, and he carried Ruth to the next bunk. She looked again and saw Edek's face. He was lying still and as straight as a post.

25 Copy out these sentences and add in the missing punctuation:

(a) Ruth cried out my mother

(b) Look it's your brother whispered Joseph

(c) I can't believe it mumbled Ruth we're all safe

(d) Just a little water said the woman

(e) The man responded she's waking up

➡ Spelling

In this chapter you will go over the rules you have learnt in Chapters 1 to 4. They relate to words ending in the suffixes -ation and -ly, homophones and commonly misspelt words.

26 Add -ation to these words and then use them in a sentence. Be careful with your spelling.

(a) accuse   (c) conserve   (e) organise

(b) perspire   (d) inform

27 Write a homophone for each of these words. Then write a sentence for each pair of words.

(a) piece   (c) mail   (e) missed

(b) groan   (d) fair

28 Copy out this passage, correcting the spelling mistakes. Use a dictionary if you need to.

Learning spellings is actualy done very easely. Find a quite place to work, a libery or a particuler spot were you will not be disterbed. Experement with diffrent ways to practise the words. You might be serprised how quickley you can pick up knew spellings. Imagen a time when spellings are your favorite activity.

➡ Vocabulary

When you are writing, it is important to convey how your characters are feeling. Here are some words that convey feelings of sadness or happiness:

sad	melancholy	sombre	wistful	despondent
mournful	gloomy	glum	dejected	frowning

happy	elated	joyous	exultant
gleeful	upbeat	optimistic	smiling

29 Write two descriptions, one of a happy character and one of a sad character. Try to use the words listed above in your descriptions, along with other words for happy and sad that you know or have looked up.

➔ Writing

In this section you will revisit the four writing styles you have already attempted: description, continuing a story, scripts and story writing.

Remember:

- Descriptions should include a range of vocabulary and use similes, metaphors and other interesting language choices.

- Continuing a story requires you to look carefully at the story you are continuing. Check which tense and person it is written in, keep the setting and characters the same and look for clues about what could happen next.

- When you write a script, remember to include plenty of stage directions and to set it out correctly without speech marks.

- When you write a story, remember to use your ideas to make a plan. Make sure your story contains an interesting or an exciting event, and 'show don't tell' so that the reader can work things out for themselves.

Now try these tasks.

30	Write a description of a calm, peaceful place. It can be real or imagined.
31	Continue the story of Ruth and her family that you read on pages 50–51.
32	Write a script about two people who are hiding.
33	Write a short story set in a secret place.

Full steam ahead

Train journeys may be an everyday event but trains and train travel can be the basis for great stories and other texts. The beautiful scenery through the window makes for vivid descriptions, the people on the train can inspire interesting characters and the mechanics of these machines provide plenty of material for non-fiction writing. The sounds and sights on board a train can sweep you away to other places and times. What adventures will you create while on the move?

Skill focus: Inference

In this chapter you will practise your inference skills. You will learn how to spot clues about the way a character is feeling, what they might be thinking or why they are doing what they are doing.

A reading list of stories and non-fiction books about trains, train journeys and railway stations can be found in *English Year 4 Answers*.

→ Comprehension

When you are reading a text, the characters do and say things that show how they are feeling and what they are thinking. The text won't always say outright what the character is thinking, but the clues will be there. For example, rather than, 'Nikita was confused', you will see clues such as, 'She frowned and looked again', or, 'Her forehead wrinkled as she peered closer at the letter, trying to make sense of the words'.

■ We don't need to be told this girl is confused. We can tell by the expression on her face. It is the same when we read a text, except the clues come from the words in the text.

The word 'confused' is not written but you can use your knowledge of how people behave in real life to help you work out that Nikita is confused.

Questions that ask you to infer how characters are feeling may look like this:

- How did the character feel when ...?
- What was the character thinking about when ...?
- Why do you think the character ...?
- Why did the character ...?

You may be asked to give evidence to back up your answer. This means you will need to quote from the text or refer to things the character does or says.

Take a look at the following example:

As the audience began to applaud and the red curtain swept aside, Freya was almost blinded by the stage lights. Her knees were still quivering and her throat was so dry that she thought the words might refuse to come out of her mouth. This was her first starring role and she knew the hall was full. In the audience, she could just make out the broad grins on the faces of her parents and her little sister, Jen. Her parents were wide-eyed and sitting up tall, their gaze glued on the stage. Jen, as always, was fidgeting on her seat and fiddling with her phone. Typical!

1 How do you think Freya is feeling at the start of the passage? Give a reason for your answer. (2 marks)

To work out how Freya is feeling, you need to find out what she is doing and thinking. The clues are highlighted in yellow for you. Now, think about real life and when people might do and think these kinds of things. How would they be feeling? Your answer might look like this:
I think Freya is feeling nervous (1 mark) because her 'knees were still quivering and her throat was so dry' (1 mark).

2 How do you think Freya's parents are feeling in the passage? Refer closely to the text in your answer. (3 marks)

Now you need to find clues about her parents. Look at what they are doing and the expressions on their faces. Think about real life and what expressions like these tell you about how people are feeling.

3 What do you think Jen is thinking at the end of the passage? Why do you think this? (2 marks)

Follow the same steps to answer this question, but you need to focus on what Jen is thinking rather than what she is feeling. Think about her age and who she is as this might also be important.

> Now try to answer questions 2 and 3 yourself.

Try this comprehension exercise, using the guidance above to help you answer the questions. Inference questions are in bold.

The Railway Children

When their father is wrongfully accused of being a spy and sent to prison, Roberta, Peter and Phyllis are forced to move to Yorkshire with their mother. In the quiet countryside they have only the sound of the passing trains to remind them of the life they once enjoyed in the city.

After the adventure of Peter's coal-mine, it seemed well to the children to keep away from the station – but they did not, they could not, keep away from the railway. They had lived all their lives in a street where cabs and omnibuses[1] rumbled by at all hours, and the carts of butchers and bakers and candlestick makers (I never saw a candlestick
5   maker's cart; did you?) might occur at any moment. Here in the deep silence of the sleeping country the only things that went by were the trains. They seemed to be all that was left to link the children to the old life that had once been theirs.

Straight down the hill in front of Three Chimneys the daily passage of their six feet began to mark a path across the crisp, short turf. They began to know the hours
10   when certain trains passed, and they gave names to them. The 9.15 was called the Green Dragon. The 10.7 was the Worm of Wantley. The midnight town express, whose shrieking rush they sometimes woke from their dreams to hear, was the Fearsome Fly-by-night. Peter got up once, in chill starshine, and, peeping at it through his curtain named it on the spot.

15   It was by the Green Dragon that the old gentleman travelled. He was a very nice-looking old gentleman, and he looked as if he were nice, too, which is not at all the same thing. He had a fresh-coloured, clean-shaven face and white hair, and he wore rather odd-shaped collars and a top-hat that wasn't exactly the same kind as other people's. Of course the children didn't see all this at first. In fact the first thing they
20   noticed about the old gentleman was his hand.

'The Green Dragon's going where Father is,' said Phyllis; 'if it were a really real dragon, we could stop it and ask it to take our love to Father.'

'Dragons don't carry people's love,' said Peter, 'they'd be above it.'

'Yes, they do, if you tame them thoroughly first. They fetch and carry like spaniels,'
25 said Phyllis, 'and feed out of your hand. I wonder why Father never writes to us.'

'Mother says he's been too busy,' said Bobbie; 'but he'll write soon she says.'

'I say,' Phyllis suggested, 'let's all wave to the Green Dragon as it goes by. If it's a magic dragon, it'll understand and take our love to Father. And if it isn't, three waves aren't much. We shall never miss them.'

30 So when the Green Dragon tore shrieking out of the mouth of its dark lair, which was the tunnel, all three children stood on the railing and waved their pocket-handkerchiefs without stopping to think whether they were clean handkerchiefs or the reverse[2].

And out of a first-class carriage a hand waved back. A quite clean hand. It held a newspaper. It was the old gentleman's hand.

35 After this it became the custom for waves to be exchanged between the children and the 9.15.

And the children, especially the girls, liked to think that perhaps the old gentleman knew Father, and would meet him and tell him how his three children stood on a rail far away in the green country and waved their love to him every morning, wet or fine.

Slightly adapted from *The Railway Children* by E. Nesbit

[1] omnibus = the old-fashioned word for a bus
[2] reverse = opposite

4 Look at the first paragraph. What is the main difference between where the children used to live and where they live now? (2 marks)

5 'they could not ... keep away from the railway' (line 2). What does this tell you about the children? (2 marks)

6 Why do you think the children thought the man was a 'nice-looking' gentleman (lines 15–16)? (1 mark)

7 'the Green Dragon tore shrieking out of the mouth of its dark lair' (line 30). Why do you think the author described the tunnel like this? (2 marks)

8 How do you think the children feel about their father? How do you know? Give two ideas and two reasons. (4 marks)

9 What do you think about Peter? What kind of boy is he? Choose two words to describe him and give a reason from the text for each. (4 marks)

Speaking and listening

10 Take turns to sit in the 'hot seat' at the front of the room as one of the characters from *The Railway Children*. Answer questions from your classmates. When it is your turn to ask the character some questions, try to think about his or her feelings during the scene in the passage.

Now try this comprehension exercise. It is based on a non-fiction text about the history of trains.

Steaming ahead

Trains are a part of our everyday life now, but how did they become such an important way of travelling?

Horses, oxen or people provided the pulling power for cars on rails and roads for thousands of years. In the 1800s, inventors came up with an alternative. They worked out how to use steam power for pulling wheeled vehicles. In 1825, the world's first public steam railway, the 25-mile long Stockton and Darlington line, opened in
5 England. On its opening day, the train hauled both freight and passenger cars. Later, it was used mainly for carrying coal. Five years later, the Liverpool and Manchester line opened with its new, steam-driven passenger trains. The company had run a competition called the Rainhill Trials to find the best locomotive for its railway. Both horse-drawn and steam locomotives took part. The steam-driven *Rocket* won.

10 The success of the *Rocket* convinced investors to back the development of steam-powered locomotives. The brains behind the *Rocket* and the Stockton and Darlington and Liverpool and Manchester railways were George Stephenson and his son Robert. In 1823, they set up the world's first locomotive factory. Other British engineers began to experiment with steam power, and locomotives were made for use in
15 Britain and around the world.

Great moments on the railways

1769 Frenchman Nicolas Cugnot builds the first steam-powered vehicle.

1804 British engineer Richard Trevithick tests the first steam locomotive for the Penydarran Ironworks in Wales.

20 **1825** The Stockton and Darlington Railway opens in Britain – the first public railroad to use steam-powered locomotives.

1829	Robert and George Stephenson's *Rocket* wins the Rainhill Trials. It becomes the locomotive used for the Liverpool and Manchester Railway.
1840s	Semaphore signalling is introduced. The first tickets for train journeys are issued.
25 **1863**	London Underground's Metropolitan Line opens and is the world's first underground passenger railroad.
1883	The Luxurious Orient Express first runs on June 5 from Paris, France, to Bucharest in Romania.
1893 30	The New York Central and Hudson River Railroad claims that its steam locomotive No. 999 travels faster than 100mph.
1900	The Paris Metro opens.
1904	The New York City Subway opens.
1938	Mallard sets the world speed record for a steam-powered locomotive (126 mph).
1955 35	The world's most powerful single-unit diesel-electric locomotives, the Deltics, first run between London and Liverpool.
1980	The first electromagnetic trains (Maglevs) open at Birmingham Airport in Britain.
1981	TGV (*Train a Grande Vitesse*) first runs between Paris and Lyon in France.
1994 40	The Channel Tunnel is completed, linking rail networks in Britain and the Continent.
1996	A Maglev train on the Yamanashi test line in Japan reaches a staggering 350 mph.

■ The TGV still runs between many French cities. SNCF is the national train operator in France.

Slightly adapted from *All About Trains*, edited by Michael Harris

11 When did the first public steam railway open? (1 mark)

12 Why do you think inventors wanted to find different ways of pulling carriages on rails, instead of using animals or people? (2 marks)

13 Which competition did George Stephenson win and how did he win it? (2 marks)

14 (a) When and where did the first underground passenger railroad open? (1 mark)

   (b) If you want to get a train from England to France, what would you travel through? (1 mark)

   (c) Where is the fastest train mentioned in the passage? (1 mark)

15 Why do you think engineers wanted to build a railway underground? (2 marks)

16 Imagine you lived in 1825 and had the chance to travel on one of the first passenger steam trains. How do you think you would feel? Give reasons for your answer. (4 marks)

Speaking and listening

17 Do you like travelling on trains? What is your favourite way of getting about? Sailing, flying, driving or even ballooning, perhaps? Give a short speech to the class about your favourite way of travelling. Give some reasons for your choice.

➔ Grammar

In this section you will learn about different types of sentences. It is important to use a range of sentence types in your writing to make it interesting to read.

Types of sentences

There are four main types of sentence:

- **Questions**, which ask something. They need a question mark. For example: When does the train leave?

- **Statements**, which give information. They end in a full stop. For example: The train will arrive at half past six.

- **Exclamations**, which show a strong feeling or reaction. They end in an exclamation mark. For example: It's so fast!

- **Commands**, which give an order or an instruction. They might end in a full stop or an exclamation mark depending on how they are said. For example: Get off the train. Now!

18 Decide which type of sentence these are:

(a) Which carriage should we sit in?

(b) Ten trains go through this station every hour.

(c) Trains are cool!

(d) Why is the train late?

(e) Give me your ticket.

(f) The Bullet Train is the fastest train in the world.

19 Write two sentences of each type. Try to stay on the theme of trains and transport.

➡ Punctuation

In this section you will learn to use reported speech.

Reported speech

You use reported speech when you write about what people talked about but you don't use their exact words. It's as if you are a reporter, explaining what was said in your own words.

For example, the following is an example of direct speech, because the exact words that Danielle spoke are used. Danielle's words are in speech marks because she actually said them:

'Can we go to the cinema, please,' asked Danielle.

The following is reported speech because Danielle's exact words are not used. The narrator is just telling the reader what Danielle was talking about. No speech marks are used:

Danielle asked if they could go to the cinema.

You can use reported speech in your writing. It works well in newspaper reports, letters and diaries. You might also use it in stories when you want to tell the reader what a character has said but don't think their words are important enough to quote directly.

---

20 Decide if these are examples of direct or reported speech:

(a) 'Please can we ride on the steam train?' begged Kerry.

(b) Ali told everyone about his exciting trip on the train.

(c) The station manager announced that the station was closed.

(d) Kara explained, 'I bought the tickets and the train leaves at 7 a.m.'

(e) Naveed spoke to the whole class about his ambition to be a train driver.

21 Change these examples of direct speech into reported speech. Remember, you won't need any speech marks.

(a) 'When does the train to Manchester leave?' enquired Salima.

(b) Bobby told his teacher, 'I left my homework on the train.'

(c) 'This train will not stop at the next station,' stated the conductor.

(d) 'I want to design trains when I'm older,' said the girl to her mother.

(e) Jess shouted to the conductor, 'Wait, I need to get on the train!'

➡ Spelling

In this section you will look at English words that come from other languages. The English language contains many words that have been borrowed or developed from foreign or ancient languages, including French, Latin and Greek.

These spellings come from French:

- Words where the -sh sound is spelled -ch. For example: chef.
- Words where the -g sound is spelled -gue. For example: tongue.
- Words where the -k sound is spelled -que. For example: unique.

These spellings come from Ancient Greek:

- Words where the -k sound is spelled -ch. For example: scheme.

These spellings come from Latin:

- Words where the -s sound is spelled -sc. For example: science.

22 Decide whether these words come from French, Greek or Latin. Use their sounds and spellings to help you.

(a) antique	**(d)** machine	**(g)** crescent
(b) scientist	**(e)** brochure	**(h)** echo
(c) league	**(f)** character	

23 Now use each of these words in a sentence.

➲ Vocabulary

Another way to help the reader to picture what you are writing about in their mind is to describe sounds. You can use sound-related vocabulary or onomatopoeia. Onomatopoeia is when a word sounds like the noise that it describes. Here are some examples:

crash	pitter-patter	boom	roar	buzz	clatter
croaking	growl	murmur	rumble	snort	knock
tap	woof	zipped	chugged		

■ This car zooms around the track, screeching on the bends.

When you say these words out loud they sound like what they mean. Use them in your writing and look out for them when you read. You might be asked why the author uses them in a comprehension exercise.

24 Find three onomatopoeic words for each of the following categories. You could use some from the list above or think of some of your own.

(a) animal noises   **(c)** how people talk   **(e)** vehicles and transport

(b) weather   **(d)** making music

25 Now use one example from each set of onomatopoeic words in a sentence.

➲ Writing

Most often, stories are written from the point of view of the narrator, a person who is not part of the story but who tells the reader about what happened and describes things to the reader. This allows the reader to watch the story from the outside.

Sometimes a story is told by one of the characters in the story, often the main character. This allows the reader to experience events from the point of view of that character and understand their feeling and reactions to things.

When you are writing from the point of view of a particular character, you need to:

- put yourself in the character's place
- think about their feelings
- think about their opinions
- think about their relationships with other characters in the story
- think about why they do what they do.

Here is an example. Imagine you are retelling the familiar story of Cinderella from Cinderella's point of view. This part is when she arrives at the ball:

The main story has not changed.   *The character explains how she felt and reacted.*   *It is written in the first person.*

As the pumpkin carriage pulled up outside the palace, I couldn't believe how beautiful it was. So different from the dark, dusty basement I live in. I carefully stepped down from the carriage, lifting my beautiful dress slightly to stop me from tripping over it in my elegant glass slippers. For the first time in my life, I felt like a princess.

In the grand ballroom, an enormous glittering chandelier lit the room. The marble floor glistened and the sweeping staircase was covered in a luscious red carpet. Men and women, dressed in their finest clothes, floated across the dance floor in pairs and I longed to have somebody to dance with.

Common features of stories are still used, including descriptive language.

Now try the following writing tasks, using the advice above to help you write from a particular point of view.

26 Rewrite a well-known fairy tale from the point of view of the main character. Choose a fairy tale you know well.

27 Imagine a typical day at school. Write about it from the point of view of a teacher.

28 Imagine going on a long train journey through a beautiful landscape, stopping at different stations. Write about it from the point of view of the train driver or the conductor.

29 Retell the passage from *The Railway Children* that you read on pages 61–62, from the point of view of one of the children in the story. You can decide which one.

Beautiful beasts

There are many beautiful beasts in our world, from the tiniest creepy crawly to the largest mammal, from creatures that live in the Arctic to creatures that live in the sea. Their different movements, colours, behaviours, sounds and lives have provided inspiration for the imaginative minds of writers and now, hopefully, they will do the same for you.

Skill focus: Author's use of language

Earlier in the book, in Chapter 4, you learnt to explain why writers choose certain words or phrases. In this chapter you will focus particularly on similes and metaphors. Remember that you are a writer too, so ideas that you see in the texts that you read are also ideas you can use in your own writing. Similes and metaphors will make your own writing more vivid and engaging.

A reading list of exciting animal stories can be found in *English Year 4 Answers*.

➜ Comprehension

A simile is a technique used by authors to tell you more about what they are describing. A simile compares two things. By using one thing to help describe another, the author can help you to see what they see in their imagination.

A **simile** uses the words 'like' or 'as' to compare two things. For example:

Eddy searched the cupboards for something to eat, **as hungry as a wolf** hunting its prey.

A wolf is a wild animal known for tearing its prey apart and devouring it hungrily. Comparing Eddy with a wolf makes him seem even hungrier and more desperate for something to eat.

Metaphors also use one thing to describe another thing but without using the words 'like' or 'as'. They just say that one thing *is* another thing. This makes the comparison even stronger. You can spot metaphors by looking for something that isn't what it actually says it is, but you know what the author means. For example:

> Glowworms, **nature's night-lights**, keeping everyone safe when the sun goes down.

This metaphor gives the reader a picture of bright lights in the darkness. Night-lights are also used to help children feel safe in the dark, making the glowworms seem like caring and unfrightening creatures.

Similes and metaphors are called 'imagery' because they give the reader an 'image' or picture in their mind to help them understand what the author is describing. Using imagery when you are writing can help to make your descriptions more effective.

You may be asked why the author has chosen to use a simile or a metaphor or you may be asked what the simile or metaphor tells you. To do this, you need to think about what is being compared to the thing that is being described.

- What thoughts enter you head when you think of the thing that is being used as a comparison?
- How does it compare to the thing being described? How does it compare in terms of, for example, size, shape, sound, smell and touch?
- What do you feel when you think of it? Do you feel, for example, scared, happy or safe?
- Finally, how does all of this information add to the description?

Here is an example:

Moon

The universe's light bulb,
Switched on to keep the dark at bay,
To light our way.
Watching the Earth,
Protecting her from nocturnal fears,
Like a midnight security guard,
Flashing his torch,
Banishing the blackness.

---

1 (a) Find and copy a metaphor from the text. (1 mark)

Look for a phrase that describes something but doesn't include the actual word for the thing being described. The phrase in yellow is a metaphor. The author means 'the moon' but says 'light bulb' because the moon is similar to a light bulb.

(b) Why has the poet chosen this metaphor? (2 marks)

For this question, you need to think about why a light bulb is similar to the moon. Think about the shape of a light bulb, what it looks like and what it does. Imagine a light bulb and a moon in your mind and think about the similarities. The question has 2 marks, which means you need to think of two ways in which the moon and a light bulb are similar. Your answer might look like this:

The poet has chosen this metaphor because the moon glows brightly like a light bulb (1 mark). It also hangs in the sky like a light bulb hangs from the ceiling (1 mark).

2 'Like a midnight security guard'. Why is this simile effective? (2 marks)

Again, you need to think about what is being compared to a 'security guard' and why. Do the same as you did for the metaphor: imagine a security guard and think about the similarities between a security guard and the thing that is being described as a security guard.

Now try to answer question 2 yourself.

Try the following comprehension exercise, using the simple steps above to help you answer the questions. Questions about the authors' use of language are in bold.

Garden creatures

Here is a pair of children's poems about some garden beasties.

Snail

With skin all wrinkled
Like a Whale
On a ribbon of sea
Comes the moonlit Snail.
5 The Cabbage murmurs:
'I feel something's wrong!'
The Snail says: 'Shhh!
I am God's tongue.'

The Rose shrieks out:
10 'What's this? O, what's this?'
The Snail says: 'Shhh!
I am God's kiss.'

So the whole garden
(Till stars fail)
15 Suffers the passion
Of the Snail.

From *The Iron Wolf* by Ted Hughes

Woodlouse

Armoured dinosaur,
blundering through jungle grass by
dandelion-light.

Knight's headpiece, steel-hinged
5 orange-segment, ball-bearing,
armadillo drop.

Pale peppercorn, pearled
eyeball; sentence without end,
my rolling full stop.

By Judith Nicholls

3 **(a) In 'Snail', find and copy a metaphor in the first verse. (1 mark)**

(b) What is this metaphor describing? (1 mark)

(c) Why did the poet choose this metaphor? (1 mark)

4 In 'Snail', why does the cabbage think something is wrong? (1 mark)

5 In 'Snail', what does the poet mean by 'Till stars fail'? (1 mark)

6 **(a) In 'Woodlouse', list three things that the poet compares the woodlouse to in the first two verses. (3 marks)**

(b) Choose your favourite comparison and explain why you think it is so effective. (2 marks)

7 **Why does the poet compare the woodlouse to a 'pale peppercorn' (line 7)? (2 marks)**

8 Do you think Judith Nicholls likes woodlice? Give a reason for your answer. (2 marks)

Speaking and listening

9 With a partner, choose an animal you both know about. Take it in turns to compare it to something else using the phrase, 'A _____ is like a _____ because _____'. See who can come up with the most convincing similes.

Now try this comprehension exercise. It is another poetry comprehension, which is a common place to find questions about the author's use of language, especially similes and metaphors.

Creature comparisons

These poems are about some slightly larger creatures.

Lobster

This is the Lobster's song:
'Has anybody seen a
Heavy-duty knight
Dancing through the fight
5 Like a ballerina?
I was a thrilling sight!
Alas, not for long!

It was the stupid sea,
The fumbling, mumbling sea,
10 The sea that took me apart
And lost my clever wits
And lost my happy heart
And then jammed all the bits
Back together wrong.
15 Now I'm just a fright.
I don't know what to do.
I'm feeling pretty blue.'

From *The Iron Wolf* by Ted Hughes

Birds

early on the lawn
an immaculate hunter;
robin, dressed to kill

a celebrity,
5 the high-trapezing seagull
autographs the sky

sober roosting gulls
in this exotic sunset
become flamingoes

By Irene Rawnsley

10 (a) Find and copy a simile from the first verse of 'Lobster'. (1 mark)

(b) Explain why the poet chose this simile. (2 marks)

11 What does the lobster in the poem think of himself now? Give a reason for your answer from the poem. (2 marks)

12 In 'Lobster', what are the two meanings of the phrase 'pretty blue' (line 17)? (2 marks)

13 In 'Birds', why does the poet describe the robin as being 'dressed to kill' (line 3)? Give two reasons. (2 marks)

14 In 'Birds', the poet uses a metaphor in the second verse to describe the seagull. Explain how it is effective. (3 marks)

15 Why do the gulls 'become flamingoes' in the third verse of 'Birds'? (2 marks)

Speaking and listening

16 Choose one of the poems you have read in this chapter and learn it by heart. Perform it to your class. You might like to perform alone, or practise and perform with a partner or in a small group.

→ Grammar

You can make the descriptions in your own writing more vivid and exciting by using similes and metaphors.

Similes and metaphors

When you are describing something in words, it is useful to give the reader ways to imagine what you are writing about. If you want them to imagine what the sky looks like, for example, you can tell them about other things that are similar to the type of sky in your story.

Similes do this using the words 'like' or 'as'.

For example, if the sky is bright blue on a warm day, you might say:

> The sky was like a thick, cosy, blue blanket.

It is a nice day, which people will enjoy, so you can compare it to something comforting like a warm blanket.

For example, if the sky is dark and stormy on a winter's day, you might say:

> The sky was as dull as a rusty, tin roof.

This is an unpleasant day, with bad weather, so it should be compared to something that is not so nice.

If you really want to help the reader see the sky as you see it in your imagination, extend the simile further. For example:

> The sky was like a thick, cosy, blue blanket, **keeping the whole world warm and safe.**

> The sky was as dull as a rusty, tin roof **that let in the rain.**

You could also try using a metaphor. To create a metaphor, you use one thing to help describe another, as in a simile, but you don't use the words 'like' or 'as' to help you do it. This makes the two things sound more similar. It really helps the reader to understand what you are describing, but metaphors are harder to think of. For example:

> A deep blue blanket covered the earth.

> The world was enclosed by a rusty roof, full of holes where the rain leaked through.

Look out for metaphors when you are reading, to help you become familiar with what they are.

---

17 Decide whether these are similes or metaphors:

(a) Mist rose from the forest like a boiling kettle.

(b) The green forest giants guarded the animals below.

(c) The canopy was an umbrella of leaves.

(d) The blossoming flowers opened like umbrellas.

(e) The tree trunk was as straight as a ruler.

18 Complete these similes. Try to make them longer than just a simple comparison.

(a) The cheetah was as fast as ...

(b) The forest was as dark as ...

(c) The water glistened in the sunlight like ...

(d) The forest was packed with trees like ...

(e) The boulders were piled high like ...

➲ Punctuation

In this section you will learn to use exclamation marks accurately. It is important to use them properly, because they lose impact if you overuse them.

Exclamation marks

Exclamation marks:

- are used singly – never use more than one at once
- are used instead of a full stop at the end of a sentence
- show something was shouted or said loudly
- show strong feelings or emotions
- show the reader that something important, exciting or surprising is happening
- go inside the speech marks if you use them when someone is speaking.

For example:

Ouch! That really hurt.

The teacher bellowed, 'Sit down!'

19 Copy out these sentences, adding the missing exclamation marks:

   (a) Help me.

   (b) 'What a mess.' yelled my brother.

   (c) Amazing. We could finally see the ocean.

   (d) I protested, 'It's not fair.'

   (e) Wow.

20 Copy out these sentences, filling in the gaps between the speech marks so that an exclamation mark is needed:

   (a) '_____!' hollered the girl's friend.

   (b) The teacher exclaimed, '_____!'

   (c) '_____!' she called.

   (d) Aaron shouted, '_____!'

   (e) '_____!' exclaimed the policewoman.

➲ Spelling

In this section you will learn how to spell words that end in the sound '-shn'. The following suffixes are used to spell the sound '-shn':

- -tion (this is the most common way to spell the sound 'shn')
- -ssion
- -sion
- -cian.

You need to look at the end of the root word to work out which ending to use. The root word is the original word that the new word is made from.

- If the root word ends in -t or -te, use -tion. For example:

    inject ⟶ injec**tion**

    hesitate ⟶ hesita**tion**

- If the root word ends in -ss or -mit, use -ssion. For example:

  express ⟶ expre**ssion**

  ad**mit** ⟶ admi**ssion**

- If the root word ends in -d or -se, use -sion. For example:

  expand ⟶ expan**sion**

  ten**se** ⟶ ten**sion**

- If the root word ends in -c or -cs, use -cian. For example:

  musi**c** ⟶ musi**cian**

  mathemati**cs** ⟶ mathemati**cian**

---

21 Add the correct ending to turn these root words into new words. Choose either -tion, -ssion, -sion or -cian. Use the examples above to help you.

(a) act   **(e)** permit   **(i)** magic

(b) invent   **(f)** comprehend   **(j)** politics

(c) complete   **(g)** extend

(d) confess   **(h)** electric

22 Now use each word in a sentence.

⮕ Vocabulary

In this section you will practise creating more similes, which you learnt how to do earlier in the chapter. Remember, a simile is a way to describe something by comparing it with something similar using the word 'like' or 'as'.

It is important to choose the right comparison. To help you do this, think about the following:

- Do the two things you want to compare look similar? Do they have a similar shape, colour, height or texture?

- Do the two things you want to compare sound similar?

- Do the two things you want to compare make you feel similar? Do they both make you feel happy, sad or scared?
- Do the two things you want to compare both fit comfortably into the setting of your piece of writing? For example, comparing a beautiful rushing river to a fast car seems odd because the river is part of the natural world and has been around for centuries and the car is man-made and modern.
- Are the two things you want to compare almost the same? If so, the comparison won't work. For example, the comparison in 'the car was as fast as a motorcycle' doesn't add much to the reader's understanding because motorcycles are so similar to cars in terms of their speed and how they move.

---

23 Copy and complete these similes.

(a) The elephant was as heavy as ...

(b) The monkeys chattered like ...

(c) The lagoon was as blue as ...

(d) The birds were brightly coloured like ...

(e) The trees were as straight and tall as ...

24 Write similes for the following nouns. You can choose any element to describe.

(a) lake   (c) tiger   (e) crocodile

(b) sun   (d) snake

➔ Writing

In this chapter you are going to write your own animal poems describing a particular animal or group of animals.

There are a few differences between writing poetry and other types of writing:

- Poems often contain lots of descriptive language, including similes and metaphors.

- The description in poetry is often very tightly packed in. This means that every word is more important than it is normally and less important words are sometimes missed out.

- Poems are written in lines, which are sometimes grouped together into verses. Sometimes the lines are short; sometimes they are longer.
- Poems might not be written in full sentences.
- The poet can choose when to end one line and start a new line.
- The poet can choose how to punctuate the poem. They might use capital letters, commas and full stops, or they might not.
- A poem can rhyme or have a particular rhythm (beat), but it does not have to.

You can plan a descriptive poem by brainstorming everything you know about the subject of the poem. What does it look like? What does it sound like? What does it smell like? What do people think about it? What is it known for? For example:

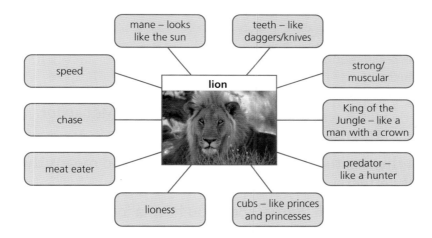

Decide what the aim of your poem is. Do you want the lion to seem dangerous or wild or beautiful? Now choose the ideas from the spider diagram that meet this aim and use them in your poem. Once the reader has read your poem, they should have a vivid picture of a lion in their mind's eye and a clear understanding of what a lion is like.

It is really important to remember that poetry doesn't always work the first time you write it. You may need to change the order of lines, improve specific lines or words, add or take things away. Editing is very important in poetry. You should do a draft, or several drafts, before finalising your poem.

Here is an example:

Lines of different lengths   Punctuation to create pauses

Lion
Striding through the jungle like an athlete,
The lion always wins the race,
As he chases his prey,
Galloping after his supper,
The King of the Jungle will be triumphant.
Keen to feed his queen and princes,
With fresh meat,
To eat.
After dinner, he sits in the sun,
His golden crown of hair,
Frames his face like a picture,
His razor sharp teeth glisten like knives,
As he sleeps in the sun.

Simile   Metaphor

Note that the poem doesn't rhyme and it doesn't have to. Sometimes, trying to make a poem rhyme limits the words you can use and means the poem ends up being less effective.

Now try these tasks yourself. Remember, you have a lot of freedom when you write a poem, so experiment and have fun.

> **25** Choose an animal you know a lot about and write a descriptive poem about it.
>
> **26** Write a poem about a zoo. Think about all of the different animals there are in a zoo and how you can use similes (or metaphors) to describe them.
>
> **27** Write a poem about an animal using onomatopoeia. Think about the sounds the animal makes and the sounds of its habitat.
>
> **28** Write a rhyming poem about an animal.

Taking out the trash

When it comes to reading and writing, waste isn't just a load of old rubbish. Great treasures can be found at rubbish tips, at the back of the cupboard and hidden away in rickety old sheds. There is something beautiful and satisfying about recycling an unwanted item into something useful or valuable. Use some of these ideas to inspire you to put pen to paper.

Skill focus: Word meaning in context

Sometimes, when you read, you will come across new words that you haven't seen before. In this chapter, you will learn how to work out the meaning of words you don't know.

> ✳ A reading list of books about rubbish that definitely aren't rubbish and some 'cli-fi' (climate fiction) books can be found in *English Year 4 Answers*.

⊙ Comprehension

We all come across new words – even adults! There isn't always a dictionary close at hand so it is important to have ways of working out what words you don't know might mean so that you can keep on reading. In comprehension exercises, you are often asked to give definitions for words used in the passage. These questions might look like this:

- Give an alternative word or phrase for ...
- Give a definition for ...
- What does ... mean, as used in the passage?
- What is the meaning of the following words, as used in the passage?

Usually, questions like this will tell you which paragraph or line the word can be found in and this is very useful. You should:

- find the word in the passage
- read around the word: read the sentence it appears in, and also the sentence before and the sentence after
- think about what is happening in the passage at this point
- consider what word might fit in place of the word you are looking at.

The meaning of the word may now be clear to you. If not, try this:

- Look at the spelling of the word.
- Does it have an ending or a beginning that gives you a clue about what it means? For example, words ending in -ing and -ed tend to be verbs, and words beginning in un- mean the opposite of something.
- Do you recognise any part of the word? Does it come from another word you do know?

If it's still not yet clear what the word means:

- Look at where it falls in the sentence. Does its position suggest that it is a verb, an adjective or a noun?
- Use this to help you figure out what the word means. For example, if it is an adjective, what is it describing and can you use other nearby words to work out what the thing it is describing is like? If it is a verb, who is doing it and what do you expect them to be doing?

Hopefully, by now you have enough clues to have a good attempt at guessing the meaning of the word. Don't worry about being wrong. It's always better to put something, rather than nothing.

Have a look at this example:

> The hallway was **crammed** with hundred of boxes. They **teetered** dangerously, threatening to fall over at any second. Moving house was exhausting, but **discarding** all of the rubbish that had built up in cupboards and drawers felt good. Donating all of her old toys and clothes to charity had made Molly feel very **virtuous** and now it was time for a fresh start. A new adventure.

1 Give a definition for the word 'crammed' in line 1. (1 mark)

As the word comes after 'was' it is likely to be an adjective. It describes the hallway and the hallway has hundreds of boxes in it. How would you describe a hall with hundreds of boxes in it? Your answer might look like this:

Crammed means 'very full' or 'crowded'. (1 mark)

2 What is the meaning of the following words, as used in the passage?

(a) teetered (line 1) (1 mark)

-ed suggests a verb and the boxes that are about to fall over are doing it.

(b) discarding (line 2) (1 mark)

-ing suggests a verb and it is what you do to rubbish.

(c) virtuous (line 4) (1 mark)

-ous suggests an adjective and it describes how somebody felt after giving things to charity.

Try to answer question 2 by yourself.

Now try this comprehension exercise, using the simple steps above to help you answer the questions. Questions about word meaning in context are in bold.

Stig of the Dump

Barney has fallen down a cliff and a mysterious character has come to his rescue.

Something, or Somebody, had a lot of **shaggy** black hair and two bright black eyes that were looking very hard at Barney.

'Hullo!' said Barney.

Something said nothing.

5 'I fell down the cliff,' said Barney.

Somebody grunted.

'My name's Barney.'

Somebody-Something made a noise that sounded like 'Stig'.

The Thing sitting in the corner seemed to be interested. It got up and moved towards
10 Barney into the light. Barney was glad to see it was Somebody after all.

'Funny way to dress though,' he thought, 'rabbit skins round the middle and no shoes
or socks.'

'Oh puff!' said Barney, 'I can't reach my feet. You do it, Stig!'

He handed the knife to Stig.

15 Stig turned it over and felt it with his strong hairy hands, and tested the edge with a
thumb. Then instead of trying to cut the creepers he **squatted** down on the ground
and picked up a broken stone.

He's going to sharpen the knife, thought Barney.

But no, it seemed more as if he was sharpening the stone. Using the hard knife to
20 chip with, Stig was carefully **flaking** tiny splinters off the edge of the flint, until he
had a thin sharp blade. Then he sprang up, and with two or three slashes cut through
the creeper that tied Barney's feet.

Barney sat up. 'Golly!' he said. 'You *are* clever! I bet my Grandad couldn't do that, and
he's *very* good at making things.'

25 Stig grinned. Then he went to the back of the cave and hid the broken knife under a
pile of rubbish.

'My knife!' **protested** Barney. But Stig took no notice. Barney got up and went into
the dark part of the cave.

He'd never seen anything like the collection of bits and pieces, odds and ends, bric-a-
30 brac and old brock, that this Stig creature had lying about his den. There were stones
and bones, fossils and bottles, skins and tins, stacks of sticks and hanks of string. There
were motor-car tyres and hats from old scarecrows, nuts and bolts and bobbles from
brass bedsteads. There was a coal scuttle full of dead electric light bulbs and a basin with
rusty screws and nails in it. There was a pile of bracken and newspapers that looked as if
35 it were used for a bed. The place looked as if it had never been given a tidy-up.

'I wish I lived here,' said Barney.

Stig seemed to understand that Barney was **approving** of his home and his face lit up.
He took on the air of a householder showing a visitor round his property, and began
pointing out some of the things he seemed particularly proud of.

40 First, the plumbing. Where the water dripped through a crack in the roof of the cave
he had wedged the mud-guard of a bicycle. The water ran along this, through the
tube of a vacuum-cleaner, and into a big can with writing on it. By the side of this
was a plastic football carefully cut in half, and Stig dipped up some water and offered

it to Barney. Barney had swallowed a mouthful before he made out the writing on the
45 can: it said WEED KILLER. However, the water only tasted of rust and rubber.

It was dark in the back of the cave. Stig went to the front where the ashes of a fire
were smoking faintly, blew on them, picked up a book that lay beside his bed, tore
out a page and rolled it up, lit it at the fire, and carried it to a lamp set in a **niche** in
the wall. As it flared up Barney could see it was in fact an old teapot, filled with some
50 kind of oil, and with a bootlace hanging out of it for a wick.

In the light of the lamp Stig went to the very back of the cave and began to thump the
wall and point, and explain something in his strange grunting language. Barney did
not understand a word but he recognised the tone of his voice – like when grown-ups
go on about: 'I'm thinking of tearing this down, and building on here, and having this
55 done up …' Stig had been digging into the wall, enlarging his cave. There was a bit
of an old bed he had been using as a pick, and a baby's bath full of loose chalk to be
carried away.

Barney made the interested sort of noises you are supposed to make when people
tell you they are going to put up plastic wallpaper with pictures of mousetraps on it,
60 but Stig reached up to a bunch of turnips hanging from a poker stuck in the wall. He
handed Barney a turnip, took one for himself, and began to eat it. Barney sat down
on a bundle of old magazines done up with string and **munched** the turnip. The
turnip at least was fresh, and it tasted better to him than the cream of spinach he'd
hidden under his spoon at dinner time.

65 Barney looked at Stig. Funny person to find living next door to you, he thought.

From *Stig of the Dump* by Clive King

---

3 List five things that Barney sees in Stig's den. (5 marks)

4 Do you think Barney likes Stig's den? Give a reason for your answer.
(2 marks)

5 Give another word for the following, as used in the passage:

(a) shaggy (line 1) (1 mark)   (e) approving (line 37) (1 mark)

(b) squatted (line 16) (1 mark)   (f) niche (line 48) (1 mark)

(c) flaking (line 20) (1 mark)   (g) munched (line 62) (1 mark)

(d) protested (line 27) (1 mark)

6 Take it in turns to sit in a chair at the front of the class as either Stig or Barney from *Stig of the Dump*. Invite the rest of the class to ask you questions about how you felt during your first meeting at Stig's den. Try to answer in character.

Now try this comprehension activity. It is based on a non-fiction text.

Waste

Here is an article containing some excellent advice about how to reduce the amount of waste you produce.

In 2014 UK householders threw away the **equivalent** of 2.6 million double-decker buses full of rubbish (nearly 22.5 million
5 tonnes). We all produce waste but there are things we can do to **minimise** how much and what impact it has on our surroundings. Environmental groups tell us the
10 way to achieve this is to 'reduce, reuse and recycle'.

A large amount of the contents of our bins is packaging which we 'buy' at the supermarket. In the UK

■ Our beaches are polluted with rubbish that has not been disposed of properly.

15 in 2014 we produced the equivalent weight of 450 jumbo jets per week in packaging waste. Next time you are shopping, think carefully about how you can reduce your packaging:

● take your own shopping bags so you need fewer plastic carrier bags

● buy larger containers. One larger container uses less packaging (and less energy to produce) than two small ones

20 ● when buying apples, think whether they need to be in a plastic tray and wrapped in cellophane

● buy fruit and vegetables from your local greengrocer who uses low-impact brown bags.

At home, try to think of **inventive** ways to reuse items:

25   ●   use shopping bags as bin liners

    ●   take your old magazines to the doctor's surgery or dentist

    ●   take your unwanted furniture, books and clothes to a charity shop (make sure they are clean)

    ●   use both sides of the paper in your computer printer (if you really need to print)

30   ●   use plastic tubs such as margarine containers to store things or make plant pots.

More and more local councils are providing good sites for recycling a whole variety of goods, but there are also some things you can do at home:

    ●   find out where your nearest recycling point is and what they can take – cans, glass, plastic, newspapers, cardboard, shoes, old clothes

35   ●   do some research and find out which recyclable items your rubbish collectors will take

    ●   compost all of your vegetable waste, but also small quantities of shredded cardboard, bedding from your pet rabbit or hamster, and grass and **prunings** from the garden.

40   All of this can make a difference: recycling just one glass bottle will save enough energy to power a television for over one hour; if collected properly, waste oil from car oil changes could supply the annual energy needs of 1.5 million people; recycling aluminium cans saves 95% of the energy used in making a new can.

Sources: www.wasteonline.org.uk and the Scottish Oil Care Campaign

---

7 What is the purpose of this text? (1 mark)

8 What are the three main ways the writer suggests we can create less waste? (3 marks)

9 Give a definition for the following words, as used in the passage:

    (a) equivalent (line 2) (1 mark)   **(c)** inventive (line 24) (1 mark)

    (b) minimise (line 7) (1 mark)   **(d)** prunings (line 38) (1 mark)

10 Think of a new title for this passage. (1 mark)

11 Why does the author use bullet points? (1 mark)

Speaking and listening

12 Work in groups of three or four. Read the article 'Waste' and then put together a short presentation for the class about how to look after the environment by recycling and being careful with litter.

→ Grammar

In order to make your writing link together and flow well, you can use joining words called conjunctions. They are like signposts for the reader, pointing out what is coming next.

Conjunctions

Conjunctions (sometimes known as connectives) are used to join sentences and ideas together. Some link ideas that are similar and some link ideas that are different. For example:

Similar: It rained all day **so** we did not go to the park.

Different: It rained all day **but** we went to the park anyway.

Here are some more conjunctions:

For similar ideas	For different ideas
and	but
therefore	however
in addition	nonetheless
so	although
because	despite
as well as	whereas

13 Copy out these sentences and underline the conjunctions.

(a) The milk went sour so I threw it away.

(b) I like Mondays because I have my judo lesson after school.

(c) Some teachers give lots of homework whereas others give less.

(d) I like reading stories but poems are even more interesting.

(e) We had fun at the beach despite the strong winds.

14 Here are some pairs of sentences. Link them together with a conjunction to make one sentence.

(a) I don't like football. I don't like rugby.

(b) The sea was calm. I went swimming.

(c) I love reading. My brother prefers movies.

(d) Maths is interesting. English is my favourite subject.

(e) We throw too much away. We should recycle more.

15 Write your own sentences, using the conjunctions below:

(a) despite   (c) but   (e) whereas

(b) as well as   (d) although

➜ Punctuation

In this section you will practise using question marks. They are not difficult to use, but many people forget them.

Question marks

A question mark is used at the end of a sentence when the sentence is a question. This means that a question mark shows that something is being asked. The question may or may not require an answer. For example:

I heard a funny noise. Mum, is that you?

What does it mean to be brave?

A good clue to help you decide if you need to use a question mark or not is to look for a question word such as:

who   when   why
what   where   how

You can also look out for words that show somebody wants something, such as:

would   should   shall
could   can

■ How often is the rubbish collected?

Questions don't have to be full sentences. They can just be one or two words, if that word requires a response or is suggesting that the speaker is unsure about something. For example:

Really?   Me?   Sure?   Mum?

16 Copy out the following sentences, adding either a full stop or a question mark to each.

(a) He wondered if he would ever finish his book

(b) When does the film start

(c) You forgot your homework. Really

(d) Do you need that

(e) Would you like some milk

17 Here are some answers. Write what you think the question might have been. Be imaginative!

(a) 75

(b) Three and a half hours

(c) Roald Dahl

(d) Australia

(e) No thank you.

⊃ Spelling

In this section you will look at words that are spelled with the letters -ei or -ie. There is a well-known rule:

-i before -e, except after -c

However, there is a very important exception to this rule! The rule only applies when the -ei or -ie makes the sound 'ee'.

Here are some examples:

receive   The sound is 'ee' and the letters come after a -c so the rule applies.

ancient   The sound is not 'ee' so the rule does not apply.

There are also a few more exceptions, where the sound is 'ee' but the rule doesn't apply. You just have to remember these:

protein   caffeine   seize

Also:

either and neither (depending on how you pronounce them)

---

18 Fill in the missing letters in these words:

(a) bel _____ f (something you trust in)

(b) c _____ ling (what you see when you look up in a room)

(c) bel _____ ve (to think something is right)

(d) ach _____ ve (to earn something)

(e) th _____ f (someone who steals)

(f) p _____ ce (a part of something)

⊃ Vocabulary

When writing on the topic of waste and recycling, you may need to refer to the cleanliness of things. Here is some adventurous vocabulary on that subject:

| hygienic | spotless | soiled | grubby | sterile | unblemished |
| immaculate | grimy | unsanitary | squalid | pure | contaminated |

19 Find the words at the bottom of the previous page in a dictionary. Then sort them into two groups, one for words that mean 'clean' and one for words that mean 'dirty'. Give a definition for each word.

➲ Writing

In this section you will learn to write persuasively. This means writing to convince somebody to agree with you or do something that you want them to do. There are several techniques you can use to be persuasive.

Structure your work carefully:

- Start by stating your point of view clearly.

- Explain your point of view through a series of different points. Give examples or facts and figures to back up each point.

- Organise your points so that similar ideas are grouped together. This helps the reader to take your ideas on board.

- End by summarising your overall point of view again.

Use persuasive language:

- Be sure of yourself. Use phrases like: I know..., It is clear that... Evidently, ... Obviously, ... and I am certain....

- Use rhetorical questions. These are questions that don't need an answer. They will make the reader think harder about what you are saying.

- Use conjunctions to link your ideas together, just as you practised earlier in this chapter.

- Use the power of three. Describe, explain or introduce things in groups of three. For example: It is **foolish**, **selfish** and **wrong** not to recycle your rubbish.

- Use anecdotes (short, amusing stories about real events) and personal experience. Showing that you have real experience of the topic will make you sound more believable.

- Use facts and figures. If it is appropriate, use numbers and facts to back up your ideas.

- Use technical or specific vocabulary. Using vocabulary associated with the topic will make you sound like an expert.

- Use emotional language. If you can make the reader feel something, then you are more likely to convince them that your point of view is right.

Have a look at this example of an article written for a school magazine to persuade people to recycle more of their rubbish:

Clear indication of the topic

Groups of three

Rubbish! It's everywhere. At home, at school and even on the streets. It looks horrible and smells unpleasant, but there is a bigger problem brewing. The more we throw away, the more we need to produce to replace it, leading to more pollution and more depletion of fossil fuels. Frightening, isn't it? However, there is a simple solution – recycling.

Conjunctions

Technical vocabulary

Emotional language   Rhetorical question

Remember, you can be persuasive in different types of text:

- Letters: don't forget the address, date, 'Dear' and a sign off.
- Speeches: remember to address the audience directly.
- Magazine and newspaper articles: think about who will read the article and what would appeal to them.

Now try these tasks using the guidance above to help you.

20 Finish the persuasive article about recycling. Make sure you give good reasons why people should recycle and back them up with statistics and examples. You could even refer to your own home or school.

21 Write a persuasive letter to your headteacher, asking them to change something at school. It could be related to lessons, the school uniform, food or something else.

22 Imagine you are applying for your dream job. Write a letter persuading your potential new boss that you are the right person for the job.

23 Write a persuasive speech to make to your family, convincing them to waste less and recycle more at home.

Under the sea

There is an air of mystery and adventure about the watery depths of the world's seas and oceans, which make them an exciting place to read and write about. Imagine coral reefs, tropical fish, sharp-toothed sharks and even mythical sea creatures such as mermaids.

Skill focus: Summary

In this chapter you will learn how to summarise information from a text. Summarising is when you give a brief explanation of the main points of a text in your own words. This is also useful when recommending a book to a friend. You summarise when you plan a story too.

A reading list of stories set near, in or under the sea and non-fiction books about the sea and its inhabitants can be found in *English Year 4 Answers*.

➡ Comprehension

The best way to show or check that you understand something clearly is to explain it in your own words. To do this you need to use different words, which have the same meaning as the words you are summarising. These are called synonyms. If you are asked to show your summarising skills in a comprehension exercise, the question might look like this:

- Explain in your own words ...

- Describe ... using your own words ...

- Use your own words.

To answer summary questions, you need to follow a few simple steps:

- Read the question and look for a sign that you need to use your own words.
- Scan the text to find the answer.
- Think about different ways of saying the answer. Look at the keywords and find synonyms for them.
- Write the answer using different words from those used in the text.

You do not have to replace the words in the text word for word. You can change the wording entirely, as long as the meaning remains the same. For example:

> Annie looked out at the vast blue ocean. It glistened in the fading sunlight, gently rippling in the light breeze. Towards the horizon, she spied a yacht through her binoculars. It wasn't big but it was beautiful, with polished wooden sides, a crisp white sail and a chequered flag flying from the main mast. Annie dreamt of spending her life on the open seas. After many afternoons on her grandfather's boat, fishing and exploring the coves and hidden beaches, she wanted nothing more than to grow up to be a sailor.

1 Describe the sea in your own words. (3 marks)

   Find all of the information about the sea in the passage. It has been highlighted in blue for you. Use synonyms for the main words to help you describe it using your own words. Your answer might look like this:

   The sea stretched as far as the eye could see (1 mark) and it was azure (1 mark). There were very small waves (1 mark).

2 Explain, in your own words, why Annie likes the sea so much. (3 marks)

   Look for reasons why Annie likes the sea. Now think of other ways to say them. Some ideas have been highlighted in yellow to help you.

> Try to answer question 2 on your own.

Now try the following comprehension exercise, using the simple steps above to help you. Questions that ask you to summarise are in bold.

Under the water

Tom has fallen into the water and discovered a whole new world that he is gradually exploring. Here he is watching some wonderful animals pass by.

Then there came by a **shoal** of porpoises, rolling as they went – papas, and mammas, and little children – and all quite smooth
5 and shiny, because the fairies polish them every morning; and they sighed so softly as they came by, that Tom took courage to speak to them: but all they answered was,
10 'Hush, hush, hush,' for that was all they had learnt to say.

And then there came a shoal of **basking** sharks, some of them as long as a boat, and Tom was frightened at them. But they were very lazy, good-natured fellows, not greedy tyrants, like white sharks
15 and blue sharks and ground sharks and hammer-heads, who eat men, or saw-fish and threshers and ice-sharks, who hunt the poor old whales. They came and rubbed their great sides against the buoy, and lay basking in the sun with their backfins out of water and winked at Tom: but he never could get them to speak. They had eaten so many herrings that they were quite stupid; and Tom was glad when a collier brig came
20 by, and frightened them all away; for they did smell most horribly, certainly, and he had to hold his nose tight as long as they were there.

And then there came by a beautiful creature, like a ribbon of pure silver with a sharp head and very long teeth: but it seemed very sick and sad. Sometime it rolled helpless on its side; and then it dashed away glittering like white fire; and then it lay sick
25 again and **motionless**.

But one day, among the rocks he found a play-fellow. Tom had never seen a lobster before; and he was mightily taken with this one; for he thought him the most curious, odd, ridiculous creature he had ever seen. He had one claw knobbed and the other jagged; and Tom delighted in watching him hold onto the seaweed with his
30 knobbed claw, while he cut up salads with his jagged one, and then put them in his mouth, after smelling at them, like a monkey.

Adapted from *The Water Babies* by Charles Kingsley

3 Describe the basking sharks in your own words. (3 marks)

4 (a) What do you think the 'beautiful creature' in the third paragraph is? (1 mark)

(b) 'it dashed away glittering like white fire' (line 24). What technique has the author used to describe the creature? (1 mark)

5 Explain in your own words why Tom liked the lobster so much. (2 marks)

6 Give a definition for the following words, as used in the text:

(a) shoal (line 1) (1 mark)

(b) basking (line 13) (1 mark)

(c) motionless (line 25) (1 mark)

Speaking and listening

7 Imagine you are able to explore the depths of the ocean. What would it be like? Discuss it with a partner and describe what you might see.

Try this comprehension exercise. It is based on a poem.

They Call to One Another

This is a poem about the mythical creatures of the deep.

They call to one another
in the prisons of the sea
the mermen and the mermaidens
bound under lock and key
5   down in the green and salty dens
and dungeons of the sea,
lying about in chains but
dying to be free:
and this is why shortsighted men
10   believe them not to be
for down in their deep dungeons it
is very hard to see.

But sometimes morning fishermen
drag up in the net
15 bits of bright glass or the silver comb
of an old vanity set
or a letter rather hard to read
because it is still wet
sent to remind us never, never
20 never to forget
the mermen and the mermaidens
in the prisons of the sea
who call to one another
when the stars of morning rise
25 and the stars of evening set
for I have heard them calling
and I can hear them, yet.

By George Barker

8 Explain in your own words what the mermen and mermaidens wish for. (2 marks)

9 Why does the poet describe the sea as a 'prison' for the merpeople? (2 marks)

10 According to the poem, why do people not believe in merpeople? Explain using your own words. (2 marks)

11 (a) What do the fishermen find in their nets? (3 marks)

(b) Why are these objects important? (2 marks)

12 Does the poet believe in merpeople? How do you know? (2 marks)

Speaking and listening

13 Play an alliteration game. Get into pairs and decide who will play first. Player one chooses something from under the sea, like 'coral'. Player two adds a word that starts with the same sound; for example 'colourful coral'. Continue, taking it in turns to add more words. You might end up with something like: 'colossal, curious, colourful coral'.

→ Grammar

In this section you will learn how to use paragraphs effectively.

Paragraphs

A paragraph is used to group ideas in a piece of writing. There is a simple way to remember when to start a new paragraph. You should start a new paragraph when one of these things changes:

- **Topic**
- **Place**
- **Time**
- **Person** (this might be a new character arriving in the scene or a new person speaking).

You can remember this as the **Top Tip** for paragraphs.

For example:

> When James first arrived at the beach he was delighted. It was so sunny and the sand was pure white and soft between his toes. He couldn't wait to build a sandcastle. He and his brothers set out some towels and a windbreak. They took out the buckets and spades and began to dig.
>
> Several hours later, they began to get hungry. Their sandcastle was colossal. It had ten turrets, three moats and was almost as tall as Stevie, their baby brother. They took a break to have their lunch; sandwiches, juice and a piece of their favourite chocolate cake.

Time has jumped forward so a new paragraph has been used.

14 Read this passage about the sea and decide why each new paragraph has been used. Has the topic, place, time or person changed?

Ella and her dad were very excited about their fishing trip. It was all they had talked about for weeks and now the day had come. They packed up the car with rods and bait and set off for the coast.

When they arrived at the quayside, they walked along the gangplank to the little fishing boat that was to be their transport for the day. It was

103

bright blue with a small cabin and a shiny silver anchor. The boat was called *Blue Lagoon*, her named emblazoned on her stern in green paint.

Standing next to the craft was an old man with a bushy white beard. He introduced himself. 'Morning, sailors. I'm Bill, your skipper for the day.'

'Pleased to meet you,' said Dad, extending a hand in greeting. They all climbed aboard the boat and then they were off.

As the boat steered away from the quay, Ella began to think about the water and what was below them. She imagined blue whales, huge sharks, colourful fish and slimy eels.

Soon they were in open water and the land was no longer visible. Each of them chose a spot in the boat and cast their lines out into the water. Now all they had to do was sit and wait.

➔ Punctuation

In this section you will learn how to use apostrophes to show possession.

Apostrophes for possession

One reason we use apostrophes is to show possession, to show that something belongs to somebody or something. If the thing belongs to one person or thing we usually add an apostrophe and then an -s. For example:

the fin belonging to the dolphin ⟶ the dolphin's fin

the shell belonging to the crab ⟶ the crab's shell

However, if more than one person or thing owns something and therefore the noun is plural, we have to be more careful.

If the noun is plural and ends in -s, we add the apostrophe after the -s. For example:

the beaks belonging to the seagulls ⟶ the seagulls' beaks

the claws belonging to the lobsters ⟶ the lobsters' claws

If the noun is plural and doesn't end in an -s, just add an apostrophe and then an -s, as before. For example:

the spades belonging to the children ⟶ the children's spades

the nets belonging to the fishermen ⟶ the fishermen's nets

---

15 Change these phrases in the same way as in the examples above, so that you use a possessive apostrophe:

(a) the fin belonging to the shark *shark's ✓*

(b) the scales belonging to the clownfish *clownfish's*

(c) the shell belonging to the turtle *turtle's*

(d) the anchor belonging to the boat *boat's ✓*

(e) the rod belonging to the fisherman *fisherman's ✓*

16 Copy these sentences, correcting the mistakes.

(a) The dolphins' fin stuck out of the water like a warning. *dolphin's ✓*

(b) The fishermens' coats were yellow and waterproof. *Fishermen's ✓*

(c) All of the dolphin's noses poked out of the water. ✗ *noses*

(d) The eels' body was long and slimy. ✓ *eel's*

➡ Spelling

In this section you will learn about homonyms. Homonyms are words that sound the same and have the same spelling, but mean something different. For example:

I **left** the house at 3 p.m.	Take the first turning on the **left**.
The **bark** on the tree was rough.	The dog will **bark** when a visitor arrives.

Each of these words has two meanings and you need to use the meaning of the rest of the sentence to help you work out which meaning the author is using.

17 Write two definitions for each of these homonyms:

(a) bank   (d) park   (g) foot

(b) seal   (e) saw   (h) letter

(c) trip   (f) can

18 Work out which homonym fits each of these clues:

(a) When you burn wood or when you sack someone from their job.

(b) A large clawed beast of the forest or to put up with something.

(c) When two things go together or a small stick of wood used to make fire.

(d) An apartment or having a smooth, even surface.

(e) The room inside something, or the universe and other planets.

(f) To jump up high or a thin coil of metal.

➔ Vocabulary

When writing about the sea, you need to use verbs carefully. Here are some verbs to use when describing the water:

roll	undulate	crash	rumble	wash	rush	lap
swell	surge	sweep	ripple	spray	flow	

19 Use a dictionary to find the meanings of each of the verbs on the previous page.

20 Now use as many of the verbs above as you can in a short paragraph or poem about the sea.

➲ Writing

In this section you will learn to write an explanation text. This is a piece of writing that explains how something works or how something happens. It is different from an instructional text, which teaches the reader how to do something.

When you plan or write an explanation text, you should always use the following structure:

- an introduction telling the reader what the text will be about
- several paragraphs outlining clear steps in the process you are explaining
- a conclusion that reminds the reader what they now understand.

The purpose of an explanation text is to explain how something works or happens, so it is really important that your explanation is clear and you have broken up what you are explaining into small steps. You can also include a diagram or labelled picture to make it even easier for the reader to understand what you are explaining.

Using the following features will also make your explanations more effective:

- a title that shows what the text is about
- simple, formal language
- the present tense
- the third person, although the second person might be used in parts to help the reader imagine something
- vocabulary related to the specific topic, with definitions for unusual words
- conjunctions to show the order of, and links between, what you are explaining.

Here is an example of how an explanation text might begin:

This paragraph introduces the topic

A title, showing what the explanation is about

Second person used to help the reader imagine the situation

Present tense

Why does the tide go in and out?

If you stand on the beach all day and watch the sea, you will notice that at certain times of day the sea washes further up the beach. This is called the tide and it can be high (far up the beach) or low (far down the beach). The reason for these tides is found beyond the Earth.

Look up in the sky at night, and, if you're lucky, you'll see the Moon, bright and white in the sky. The Moon orbits (travels around) the Earth. It takes a month to do this. It follows a specific path because of something called gravity. Gravity is like a magnetic force between two objects, pulling them together. The Moon is pulled towards the Earth just enough to stay in orbit.

As the Earth is much bigger than the Moon, the Moon cannot pull the Earth closer to it, but it can pull the water on the Earth a little closer. On the Earth, people see this as a high tide and a low tide.

As the Moon orbits the Earth, the Earth is also spinning on its own axis once a day. As a result there are two high tides and two low tides every day.

The rest of the text is in the third person

Subject-specific vocabulary

Definitions

Conjunctions

Now try the following tasks, using the advice you have been given above. You will need to spend some time researching the topics first.

21 Write an explanation text with the title, 'How do whales and dolphins communicate with each other under the water?'

22 Choose a sea creature and write an explanation text about it. You can choose what you explain. It could be to do with survival, how it travels, or something else.

23 Write an explanation text that explains to the reader how tsunamis happen.

24 Write an explanation text to do with deep sea diving. It could be to do with how the divers use their equipment, how they recover sunken ships or something else that you are interested in.

Robots rule

Robots ... the answer to all our problems or a frightening technological nightmare in the making? Whatever you think about artificial intelligence and robotics, there is no denying that they make a great topic for a story, poem or factual article. The future is unknown but, through writing, we can begin to imagine what it might be like. How do you see our world in the future?

Skill focus: Joining the dots
In this chapter you'll get the chance to practise all the comprehension skills you have been working on in Chapters 6 to 9.

A reading list of books about robots and other exciting science fiction stories can be found in *English Year 4 Answers*.

➔ Comprehension

You have been developing the following comprehension skills:

- Inference: Remember to look at what characters do and say, and how they react to events. This will help you to work out how they are feeling and what they are thinking.

- Author's use of language: Look out for similes and metaphors. When you are explaining why the writer chose them, think about what you imagine when you read the comparison.

- Word meaning in context: Use the context, the spelling and the type of word to help you work out what new and unknown words mean.

- Summary: Find the answer in the text then use synonyms (words with similar meanings) to put it in your own words. Change the words but not the meaning.

Try this comprehension exercise. Look back at previous chapters if you need help.

The Iron Man

A huge metal monster has appeared on the clifftop.

The Iron Man came to the top of the cliff.

How far had he walked? Nobody knows. Where had he come from? Nobody knows. How was he made? Nobody knows.

Taller than a house, the Iron Man stood at the top of the cliff, on the very brink, in
5   the darkness.

The wind sang through his iron fingers. His great iron head, shaped like a dustbin but as big as a bedroom, slowly turned to the right, slowly turned to the left. His iron ears turned, this way, that way. He was hearing the sea. His eyes, like headlamps, glowed white, then red, then infra-red, searching the sea. Never before had the Iron
10 Man seen the sea.

He swayed in the strong wind that pressed against his back. He swayed forward, on the brink of the high cliff.

And his right foot, his enormous iron right foot, lifted – up, out, into space, and the Iron Man stepped forward, off the cliff, into nothingness.

15 CRRRAAAASSSSSSH!

Down the cliff the Iron Man came **toppling**, head over heels.

CRASH!

CRASH!

CRASH!

20 From rock to rock, snag to snag, tumbling slowly. And as he crashed and crashed and crashed.

His iron legs fell off.

His iron arms broke off, and the hands broke off the arms.

His great iron ears fell off and his eyes fell out.

25 His great iron head fell off.

All the separate pieces tumbled, scattered, crashing, bumping, **clanging**, down onto the rocky beach far below.

A few rocks tumbled with him.

Then

30 Silence.

Only the sound of the sea, chewing away at the edge of the rocky beach, where the bits and pieces of the Iron Man lay scattered far and wide, silent and unmoving.

Only one of the iron hands, lying beside an old, sand-logged washed-up seaman's boot, waved its fingers for a minute, like a crab on its back. Then it lay still.

35 While the stars went on wheeling through the sky and the wind went on tugging at the grass on the cliff-top and the sea went on boiling and **booming**.

From *The Iron Man* by Ted Hughes

1 At what time of day does this passage take place? (1 mark)

2 (a) What technique does the author use to describe the Iron Man's eyes (line 8)? (1 mark)

  (b) Why is this effective? (2 marks)

3 Why do you think the author chose the phrase, 'chewing away at the edge of the rocky beach' (line 31)? (2 marks)

4 Describe the Iron Man before he fell. Use your own words. (3 marks)

5 Give another word for the following, as used in the passage:

  (a) toppling (line 16) (1 mark)

  (b) clanging (line 26) (1 mark)

  (c) booming (line 36) (1 mark)

6 Explain in your own words what happened to the Iron Man when he stepped off the cliff. (2 marks)

Speaking and listening

7 Find a partner and sit back to back. One person should describe how to draw the Iron Man and the other should follow the instructions, without saying a word. See if you can communicate clearly enough with each other to create an accurate drawing.

Now try this comprehension exercise.

Robot football players

Most people have seen a game of football, and most people have seen or read about the amazing things scientists and engineers are creating with robots, but can you imagine putting the two things together?

In 1995, the little known sport of robot football was born in Korea. For over 20 years, international tournaments have been held and, just like human football,
5 there are different leagues, although in robot football they are for different sizes and shapes of robots. For example, the Hurosot league is for **humanoid** robots up to a height of 150cm and a weight of 30kg.
10 The Quadrosot league is for four-legged robots. Having started with only 38 teams participating, now over 500 teams from more than 45 countries take part.

The Robocup is played on an astroturf-like surface. There is no human involvement
15 in the game unless a robot breaks down, in which case it can be removed by a person. The size of the pitch and the ball varies depending on the size of the robots.

One large difference between robot football and human football is the absence of human error. When a robot shoots, it rarely misses! Furthermore, the robots are equally good at playing in all positions and they certainly don't argue with the referee.

20 However, robot football is not without its difficulties. The robots are programmed by humans before the match because they cannot make decisions for themselves. Their movements are jerky and quite slow. The humanoid robots also suffer a major disadvantage – they have a **tendency** to fall over once they have kicked the ball! Many robots recognise colour rather than shape so they need to know in advance
25 what colour the football will be. In contrast, when robots are able to be proper robots they are highly effective. They use a range of sensors, are shaped carefully to avoid **toppling** over and can gain **significant** speeds when moving on wheels. They can also communicate with each other via a wireless connection.

You may be wondering why robot football exists. The annual Robocup competition,
30 held in different countries around the world, states that its **mission** is to beat a team of human footballers in a traditional football match, following to the FIFA rules. They hope to achieve this goal by the year 2050. Beyond the football pitch, the technology that is developed for the Robocup can also be adapted to other, more practical, uses.

8 Why do you think robot designers want to beat human football players in the tournament? (2 marks)

9 Describe in your own words why humanoid robots find it difficult to play football. (2 marks)

10 Why are robots that aren't like humans better at football than humanoid robots? (2 marks)

11 (a) Find two examples of vocabulary that is specific to the subject of this article. (2 marks)

(b) Why did the author use technical vocabulary in the article? (1 mark)

12 Write a definition for these words, as used in the passage:

(a) humanoid (line 8) (1 mark)

(b) tendency (line 23) (1 mark)

(c) toppling (line 27) (1 mark)

(d) significant (line 27) (1 mark)

(e) mission (line 30) (1 mark)

Speaking and listening

13 How good are your listening skills? In pairs, take it in turns to pretend to be an obedient robot, which moves when told to do so by the other person. Try to think of lots of small actions that the robot must perform. Then speed up the commands and see if the robot can keep up!

→ Grammar

Answer the questions on the next page to find out what you remember about types of sentences, similes, conjunctions and paragraphs.

14 For each of the following verbs, write four sentences: a statement, a question, an exclamation and a command:

    (a) look   **(b)** listen   **(c)** think

15 Complete these similes. Try to extend them as far as possible.

    (a) The robot moved as slowly as ...

    (b) Its metal body shone like ...

    (c) His eyes glowed yellow like ...

    (d) Robots are as clever as ...

    (e) It made strange noises like ...

16 Write your own similes about the following nouns:

    (a) computer   **(c)** monster   **(e)** robot

    (b) siren   **(d)** wires

17 Copy out these sentences, adding in appropriate conjunctions:

    (a) Inventors have designed many robots _____ none are as intelligent as humans.

    (b) The robot stopped moving _____ his power source failed.

    (c) I would like a robot _____ it can do my homework.

    (d) I switched on the power _____ his lights began to flash red and blue.

    (e) My perfect robot would cook the dinner _____ do the washing up.

18 Rewrite this passage, starting a new paragraph when necessary. Then underline all of the conjunctions.

Pax 72 was the world's most loyal robot. He lived with the Hendrick family at their home, where he helped to run the household. Every day, he made delicious breakfasts, helped the children with their homework and cleaned the house while everybody was out. He was the perfect addition to the household. However, Pax wasn't very happy. He was bored, he knew he was a clever robot and he wanted to do more with his life. Every day he looked out of the window at the world beyond. A world that he had never experienced. If he could, he would have cried. Robots weren't supposed to feel emotions. Pax was different and he knew it. Just before Christmas, when Pax was wrapping the presents while the Christmas cake was baking in the oven, he overheard his family talking. 'I wonder what Pax would like for Christmas,' pondered Billy, the family's youngest son. 'Don't be silly,' replied Dad. 'Pax doesn't want presents, he's a robot.' 'Well, can we at least give him a day off?' begged Billy. 'Of course not, Christmas Day is too busy. Now that's an end to it,' stated Dad as he changed the subject. From that day on, although Pax was still sad, he knew he had a friend in Billy and he promised himself that one day he would ask Billy to help him.

➔ Punctuation

Can you remember the punctuation rules you have practised in Chapters 6 to 9? You have learnt the rules for using exclamation marks, question marks and apostrophes for possession. You have also learnt how to turn direct speech into reported speech and to punctuate it correctly. Look back at the previous chapters if you need a reminder.

19 Copy out this passage and add in the missing punctuation or change it if it is incorrect:

From the corner of the laboratory, Asha could just make out the robots outline. It was very dark and as she walked towards it, she knocked into an overturned chair. 'Ouch' she cried out, rubbing her knee. Ashas eyes were adjusting to the dark and she could see the robots flashing control panel more clearly. It was flashing red. But why. Red meant it was malfunctioning. It meant the robots main system was failing and that Ashas perfect invention was no longer perfect. Her colleagues reactions had been great when she first unveiled the robot. But now she didn't want to see everyones faces when she told them it had failed. Disaster.

20 Turn this direct speech into reported speech:

(a) 'Stop there!' shouted the scientist to the robot.

(b) The scientist wondered, 'How can I fix this?'

(c) 'If I turn off the power, everything will be fine,' said the inventor.

(d) My friend asked me, 'Would you like a robot friend?'

(e) 'In the future, the planet will be full of robots,' stated the scientist.

➔ Spelling

Now it is time to practise the spelling rules you have looked at in previous chapters. The rules you encountered related to words from other languages, -ion and -ian suffixes, -ie and -ei words and homonyms.

21 Copy out these sentences, adding a single homonym that fits into both gaps in each sentence:

(a) I _____ my book on the table on the _____ hand side of the room.

(b) The detective put the notes from the police _____ in his leather _____.

(c) Please _____ to the answer with your finger and make your _____ clearly.

(d) Make sure you _____ when the _____ flies overhead, otherwise it might fly into you.

(e) Mum left the _____ control in some _____ corner of the living room.

(f) Choose the _____ answer and tick the box _____ next to it.

(g) I found some coins on the river _____ so I took them to the _____ and put them in my account.

22 Correct the following spellings and use each word in a sentence.

(a) permision   (d) discussian   (g) hesitassion

(b) invencian   (e) comprehention

(c) magition   (f) musicion

23 Sort these words according to the language they originally came from:

tongue   science   scene   unique   machine   chemist

league   discipline   chef   echo   fascinating

24 Work out the -ei or -ie word from the clue and write it correctly:

(a) To accept or be given something

(b) To snatch or take

(c) To tell someone a lie

(d) To agree or trust in something

(e) To complete a goal or ambition

(f) A piece of paper showing what you have bought

(g) A buddy or chum

➔ Vocabulary

When you are writing about robots or other futuristic or science fiction topics, using technology vocabulary can help the reader understand your theme better. Here are some technology words that you could use:

automatic   robotic   download   hacker   password   virus   data

digital   megabyte   transmit   circuit   gadget   avatar

25 Use a dictionary to find definitions for these words.

26 Sort the words into three groups: verbs, nouns and adjectives. Some words might fit into more than one category.

→ Writing

In this section you have a chance to revisit the four writing styles you have attempted in the last four chapters: writing from different points of view, writing poetry, writing to persuade and writing to explain.

Remember:

- When writing from different points of view, you have to put yourself in the speaker's shoes. Think about their thoughts and feelings and how they would see the story.

- Poetry gives you plenty of freedom to be creative. Use lots of descriptive techniques, including similes and metaphors. You want your reader to really understand what the subject of your poem looks like, feels like or sounds like. You want the reader to feel something when they read your poem.

- Persuasive writing needs to sound confident and certain. Use a range of techniques to achieve this, including repetition, groups of three, rhetorical questions and phrases that make you sound sure of your point of view.

- Explanation texts show a reader how something works or happens. Be clear and specific, explaining each small step and including enough detail to make it easy for the reader to understand what you are explaining.

Now try these writing activities:

27 Write a story about somebody visiting our world from the future. Think about what they would think of the way we live our lives today. Would our lives seem simple and boring? Would the visitor be able to tell us about amazing technology of the future?

28 Write a descriptive poem about the future. It could be about technology, about your own future or about how our planet will look in 100 years' time.

29 Write a letter to your headteacher, persuading him or her that robot teachers would be better than real teachers and that he or she should hire robots instead of humans.

30 Choose a modern gadget or machine, find out how it works and write an explanation text about it.

Glossary

This table lists the literary, grammatical and punctuation techniques that you have come across throughout the book and briefly describes what they are.

Adjective	An adjective is a word used to describe a noun.
Adverb	Adverbs often end in -ly and describe verbs. They describe how or when something was done.
Alliteration	Alliteration is the use of a string of words that all start with the same sound.
Apostrophes for contraction	In contractions, an apostrophe is used to show where the missing letter or letters should be. For example, 'they're' is short for 'they are'.
Apostrophes for possession	In order to show that something belongs to someone or something, you need to use apostrophes. For example, 'the boy's laziness' and 'St James' Church'.
Clause	Sentences are made up of clauses. A clause is a part of a sentence with a verb in it. A single-clause sentence has one clause in it. For example: I ate my dinner. A multi-clause sentence has more than one clause in it. For example: I finished my homework and then I played netball.
Comma	A comma is a punctuation mark indicating a pause. Among its many uses are separating items in a list.
Conjunctions	Conjunctions are words (or phrases) that link ideas together and show a relationship between ideas. They include: while, moreover, however and although.
Direct speech	Direct speech is using someone's exact words in a text. This is marked using speech marks.
Exclamation marks	Exclamation marks are used at the end of sentences instead of full stops. They are used to show strong emotion, to show when something is being shouted or emphasised and at the end of single-word sentences.
First and third person	If a story is written in the first person, it means that one of the characters in the story is telling the story. If a story is written in the third person, it means it is written from the point of view of a narrator who is not part of the story.

Fronted adverbial	A fronted adverbial is a group of words acting as an adverb, modifying a verb, and placed at the start of a sentence, before a comma.
Full stop	A full stop is used to mark the end of a sentence.
Homonym	Homonyms are words that look the same but have different meanings.
Homophones	Homophones are words that sound the same but are spelled differently and have different meanings.
Metaphor	A metaphor is a phrase that describes one thing as if it were another. For example: The fence had iron teeth, keeping people away.
Multi-clause sentence	A multi-clause sentence has more than one part or idea.
Noun	A noun is the name of a person, a place or a thing. Common nouns are the general names of things. 'Hat' and 'coat' are common nouns. Proper nouns are the words for specific, one-of-a-kind places, people or things. They always begin with a capital letter. 'Anne' and 'Great Britain' are proper nouns. A collective noun is a noun for a group of similar things. For example, a group of lions is called a 'pride'. An abstract noun is a noun that you cannot experience using the five senses. For example, confusion, love and decision.
Noun phrase	A noun phrase is a phrase in which a noun is joined by adjectives (describing words), prepositions (words showing direction or position) and other nouns.
Paragraph	A paragraph is used to group ideas in a piece of writing. You should start a new paragraph when the Topic, Place, Time or Person changes.
Past tense	The simple past tense is usually formed by adding -ed to the verb. For example: I walked to the shop. The present perfect tense shows that an event has passed and finished. You use the verb 'have' before the simple past of the main verb. For example: I have walked to the shop hundreds of times in the past.
Personification	Personification is when something non-human is described as if it is human and is displaying human emotions or actions. For example: The gentle breeze tickled my skin.
Plural	When there is more than one of a noun, we use a plural version of the noun. For example, 'rabbit' becomes 'rabbits'.
Prefix	A prefix is a group of letters added to the beginning of a word.
Preposition	A preposition is a word showing position or direction. In a sentence, prepositions are found before a noun. For example, 'at' is the preposition in 'The dog barked at its owner'.

Pronoun	A word used instead of a noun. For example, he, she and it.
Question mark	A question mark instead of a full stop is used at the end of a sentence that is a question.
Reported speech	Reported speech communicates what someone said without using their exact words.
Sentence	A sentence is a group of words that are connected to each other but not to any words outside the sentence.
Simile	A simile is a phrase that compares two things using the word 'like' or 'as'. For example: The plane soared through the night sky like a shooting star.
Speech marks	Speech marks – " " or ' ' – are used to mark the words that are spoken by someone in a piece of writing like a story or a report. They are sometimes called quotation marks or inverted commas.
Suffix	A suffix is a group of letters added to the end of a word.
Synonym	A synonym is a different word with the same meaning.
Verb	A verb is an action or a doing word. For example, 'barked' is the verb in 'The dog barked at its owner'.

Index